MATERIALIEN
FÜR DIE SEKUNDARSTUFE II

DIESTERWEGS
NEUSPRACHLICHE
ARBEITSMITTEL

How to deal with texts

A systematic approach to the analysis of texts

Reinhard Kemnitz
Norbert Köhn
Friederike Poziemski
John Poziemski

DIESTERWEG

2. Auflage

Druck A [5] / Jahr 2008
Alle Drucke der Serie A sind im Unterricht parallel verwendbar.

Umschlagkonzeption: Werbeatelier Richter, Seeheim-Jugenheim
Satz: Fotosatz Otto Gutfreund, Darmstadt
Druck und Bindung: westermann druck GmbH, Braunschweig

ISBN 978-3-425-04432-3

Contents

Introduction 7
Chapter I: Text – Categories and Forms
Introductory Remarks 9
1. *Brian Morris,* Genesis 13
2. *James Thurber,* The Rabbits Who Caused All The Trouble . . . 14
3. *Edward Albee,* The Zoo Story* 15
4. *Carl Sandburg,* The Hangman at Home 16
5. *Lord Tweedsmuir,* Scotland 17
6. *Bertrand Russell,* The Science to save us from Science 18
7. *Martin Luther King,* I have a Dream 20
8. Beatable and Unbeatable 22
9. Citroën 23
10. *Brian Inglis,* Kicking the Hospital Habit 24
11. *Catherine Hughes,* The Glass Menagerie 24
12. *M. King Hubbert,* The Impact of Energy on Geological Processes 26
13. *Lucy Hodges,* Decision to give parents choice on the cane criticized as unworkable 27
14. Precautions 28
15. An Agreement 29

Chapter II: Text – Structure and Types
Introductory Remarks 31
1. *James Thurber,* The Scotty Who Knew Too Much 34
2. *Langston Hughes,* Early Autumn 35
3. *R. D. Laing,* How can she be happy 37
4. *Tom Sharpe,* Vintage Stuff* 38
5. *The Duke of Edinburgh,* New Lamps for Old 39
6. *Richard Rose,* Proud to be British 40
7. *James A. Levine,* Real Kids vs. 'The Average' Family 41
8. *J. Segal, H. Yahraes,* Bringing up Mother 42
9. *Centre for British Teachers,* Take 5 43
10. *Encyclopaedia Britannica,* Battle of Trafalgar 44

* excerpt from a complete work of the same title

Chapter III: Point of View

Introductory Remarks . . . 46
1. *Henry Fielding,* Tom Jones* . . . 48
2. *D. J. Hessayon,* Plants in the Home . . . 49
3. *William Shakespeare,* The Prologue to Romeo and Juliet . . . 50
4. *Jane Austen,* Sense and Sensibility* . . . 50
5. *Alan Sillitoe,* The Loneliness of the Long-Distance Runner* . . . 51
6. *Eudora Welty,* A Visit of Charity* . . . 52
7. *James Joyce,* A Portrait of the Artist as a Young Man* . . . 53
8. *Thomas Hardy,* A Tradition of Eighteen Hundred and Four* . . . 54
9. Royal Praise, Martina's Day . . . 54
10. *Ernest Hemingway,* Hills like White Elephants* . . . 55
11. New Year's Deadly Night of Panic . . . 56
12. *William Shakespeare,* Macbeth* . . . 57
13. *Alun Lewis,* The Lapse* . . . 58
14. *James Joyce,* Ulysses* . . . 59

Chapter IV: Plot and Characters

Introductory Remarks . . . 60
1. *Arnold Wesker,* Chips with Everything* . . . 63
2. Personal Column, Requests for Friendship . . . 65
3. *Agatha Christie,* The Mysterious Affair at Styles* . . . 66
4. *Nigel Williams,* Class Enemy* . . . 67
5. *William Golding,* Lord of the Flies* . . . 69
6. *Peter Terson,* Zigger Zagger* . . . 70
7. *Charles Dickens,* A Christmas Carol* . . . 72
8. So You Think You Could Sell? . . . 73
9. *Erskine Caldwell,* Saturday Afternoon . . . 74

Chapter V: Stylistic Devices

Introductory Remarks . . . 80
1. The Declaration of Independence* . . . 85
2. The Constitution of the United States of America* . . . 85
3. *William B. Yeats,* An Irish Airman foresees his Death . . . 86
4. The Creation of the World* . . . 86
5. *Wilfred Owen,* Anthem for Doomed Youth . . . 87
6. Myth & Fact . . . 88
7. Little by Little . . . 89
8. *William Shakespeare,* Julius Caesar* . . . 89
9. *Pink Floyd,* Another Brick in the Wall . . . 90
10. Miscellaneous . . . 91

11. In Memoriam 92
12. *Ted Hughes,* The Thought-Fox 92
13. *R. S. Thomas,* In Church 93

Glossary of theoretical terms concerned with text analysis 96
Stichwortregister zum raschen Auffinden geeigneter Redemittel . . 101
Acknowledgements 102

Abbreviations

adj. adjective – **AE.** American English – **coll.** colloquial – **comp.** compositional – **derog.** derogatory – **dial.** dialect – **e.g.** for example (Latin: *exempli gratia*) – **esp.** especially – **etc.** etcetera; and so on – **fml.** formal – **G.** German – **h.** here – **i.e.** that is (Latin: *id est*) – **math.** mathematical – **obs.** obsolete – **o.'s** one's – **o.s.** oneself – **pej.** pejorative – **pl.** plural – **sl.** slang – **socio.** sociolect – **s.o.** someone – **s.th.** something – **usu.** usually – **vulg.** vulgar

CICERO. Indeed, it is a strange-disposed time:
But men may construe things, after their fashion,
Clean from the purpose of the things themselves.

Julius Caesar, I, 3, 33–35

Introduction

Texts are what this book consists of; dealing with these texts systematically is what this book is about.

"How to deal with texts" is a text analysis workbook aimed at *Oberstufenschüler*. The intention of this project is to help students to learn how to analyse texts systematically.

The student's book is divided into five chapters, which move from the general to the more specific aspects of text study, from categorizing texts, to identifying their characteristic structural features, to more detailed analyses of style. Each chapter begins with a theoretical introduction, followed by a list of useful phrases. This list is to help the students to cope with the tasks, which are meant as guidelines to deal with the corresponding texts that form the remainder of each chapter. Ideally, this book should be worked through from beginning to end; it is, however, also possible to deal with certain chapters separately.

The texts have been selected to achieve as broad a spectrum as possible from fictional through factional to non-fictional texts, from the love poem to the advertisement, from a piece of classical drama to a set of operating instructions. They all show the interrelationship between text form, composition, language, and context of usage. Additionally they can also be used for lessons dealing with English literature, and with *Landeskunde*.

Each communication, written or oral, consists of four parts (according to a basic communications model):

Sender – Message – Code – Receiver
(author – intention – text – reader)

This book concentrates on the component of 'code', i.e. on the text as it is published in printed form. The kind of communication that takes place between author and receiver via the text is a one-way communication, as the reader has to deduce all the information on how to understand a text from the text itself. So what the reader needs first is the appropriate analytical equipment to decode the text in its various layers of meaning. Such an analysis will lead to the interpretation of what the author possibly wanted to express through/in his or her text, the question of message. It can be doubted whether any interpretation will ever completely match the author's intentions. The conditions under which the author writes his or her work and the experience that forms its basis are unique, and every attempt to take these factors into account will only lead to an 'approach' toward the real message, not to a reconstruction of the author's original intention. Various methods have been tried to achieve as comprehensive an understanding of a text as possible; but all these methods, be it the structuralist, the psychoanalytic, the Marxist, the religious, the historical, the biographical, the sociological, etc., lead to a kind of interpretative arbitrariness because of their ideological foundation. This book aims at a more objective text analysis without ideological bias.

Chapter I

Text – Categories and Forms

Introductory Remarks

Traditionally, text analysis has been concerned with the so-called central genres of the novel (or prose), poetry, and drama. Every other text form was incorporated in the collective concept of non-fiction, which has tended to be seen as second-rate and inferior, due to its alleged lack of literary creativity, aesthetic qualities and ethical profoundness. Fortunately, recent study into text analysis has upgraded non-fictional texts, while continuing to pay close attention to fictional texts.

What is a fictional text? A fictional text is a text whose characters and plot are invented. Characters, action, and setting are interrelated and interdependent; they have a specific function within this artificially constructed world which reflects a philosophy of life. Certain components, like place names for example, may be recognizable within the real world, but this is incidental and their role is a fictional one.

No text is absolutely objective. Some text forms do strive after objectivity, but the result can never be fully satisfactory. A non-fictional text is one whose prime aim is to reflect as objectively as possible an aspect or aspects of the real world. Evaluative intervention is to be avoided at all costs; balance and neutrality should be the principal characteristics of the text, information its main purpose. Again it must be pointed out that there are often discrepancies between the definition and the actual text. For, in newspaper reports and documentaries as in history books, the element of personal selection distorts the absolute objectivity. The effect on the reader can be manipulative.

Now, the first category deals satisfactorily with the traditional text forms, while the second covers such texts as technical reports, documentaries, dictionary definitions. However, a number of texts have still to be classified. This "factional" group is to be found between the above two categories with overlapping elements that merge at either end with fiction and non-fiction. Within this category we have texts with elements of fictional style and/or based on past and present reality. The common feature of every single text in this group is its evaluative character; you will always find personal opinion, whether explicit or concealed.

Useful Phrases

1. This text belongs to the group of	fictional factional non-fictional	texts.

2. This text can be classified as...

3. The text	deals with treats concerns itself with presents	an extremely topical subject.

4. The title already	indicates gives a clue as to	the subject.

5. The aim of the text is as follows:

6. The events in the text	are factually true. refer to the real world. are invented.

7. The author seeks to judge the text	objectively. subjectively.

8. The author gives	his/her own opinion on... takes sides with... remains neutral	 concerning... regarding... as to...

9. The text contains a subjective	element. evaluation. comment.

10. The author	seeks to wants to	convince the reader. make a point. establish a viewpoint.

11. The story	is constructed around a single theme. is confined to one setting. involves only a few characters. is restricted to one central aspect.

12. to stress/point out/lay emphasis on/underline

13. to illustrate with examples

14. to give reasons	for against

15. A closer examination	reveals shows	that...

16. to	return to take up	another subject

17. to	analyse a text examine	from several	standpoints angles

18. The information can be arranged under several headings.

19. to

to	pinpoint	different aspects of the text
	study	
	centre on	

1. Genesis

"Who are you?" said the Prime Minister, opening the door.

"I am God," replied the stranger.

"I don't believe you," sneered the Prime Minister. "Show me a miracle." And God showed the Prime Minister the miracle of birth.

"Pah," said the Prime Minister. "My scientists are creating life in test-tubes and have nearly solved the secret of heredity. Artificial insemination is more certain than your lackadaisical method, and by cross-breeding we are producing fish and mammals to our design. Show me a proper miracle." And God caused the sky to darken and hailstones came pouring down.

"That's nothing," said the Prime Minister, picking up the telephone to the Air Ministry. "Send up a met. plane would you, old chap, and sprinkle the clouds with silver chloride crystals."

And the met. plane went up and sprinkled the clouds which had darkened the world and the hailstones stopped pouring down and the sun shone brightly.

"Show me another," said the Prime Minister.

And God caused a plague of frogs to descend upon the land.

The Prime Minister picked up his telephone. "Get the Min. of Ag. and Fish," he said to the operator, "and instruct them to procure a frog-killer as myxomatosis killed rabbits."

And soon the land was free of frogs, and the people gave thanks to the Prime Minister and erected laboratories in his name.

"Show me another," sneered the Prime Minister.

And God caused the sea to divide.

The Prime Minister picked up his direct-link-telephone to the Polaris submarine.

"Lob a few ICBMs into Antarctica and melt the ice-cap, please, old man." And the ice-cap melted into water and the sea came rushing back.

"I will kill all the first-born," said God.

"Paltry tricks," said the Prime Minister. "Watch this." He pressed a button on his desk.

And missiles flew to their pre-ordained destinations and H-bombs split the world asunder and radio-activity killed every mortal thing.

"I can raise the dead," said God.

"Please," said the Prime Minister in his cardboard coffin "Let me live again."

"Why, who are you?" said God, closing the lid.

Brian Morris, 'Weekend Telegraph' in: *Daily Telegraph*, 29 October 1965

Genesis the first book of the Bible in which the creation of the world is described **to sneer** smile, showing contempt **test-tube** glass tube used for chemical experiments **heredity** G. Vererbung **artificial insemination** the production of new life in a way which is not natural; G. künstliche Befruchtung **lackadaisical** [lækəˈdeɪzɪkl] G. lasch **cross-breeding** G. Kreuzung **mammal** [ˈmæməl] G. Säugetier **hailstone** frozen raindrop **met. plane** metereological aeroplane **silver chloride crystal** [ˈklɔːraɪd ˈkrɪstl] G. Silberchlorid-Kristall **to descend** come down **Min. of Ag.** Ministry of Agriculture **operator** s.o. who connects telephone calls **to procure** bring about **myxomatosis** [ˌmɪksəməˈtəʊsɪs] a disease which kills rabbits **to erect** build up **link** connexion **to lob** h. send over **ICBMs** intercontinental ballistic missiles **paltry** [ˈpɔːltrɪ] worthless **pre-ordained** (esp. of God or fate) fixed in advance **asunder** [əˈsʌndə] into pieces **cardboard** thick, stiff kind of paper, used for making boxes **coffin** chest for a dead person to be buried in **lid** h. G. Sargdeckel

2. The Rabbits Who Caused All The Trouble

Within the memory of the youngest child there was a family of rabbits who lived near a pack of wolves. The wolves announced that they did not like the way the rabbits were living. (The wolves were crazy about the way they themselves were living, because it was the only way to live.) One night several wolves were killed in an earthquake and this was blamed on the rabbits, for it is well known that rabbits pound on the ground with their hind legs and cause earthquakes. On another night one of the wolves was killed by a bolt of lightning and this was also blamed on the rabbits, for it is well known that lettuce-eaters cause lightning. The wolves threatened to civilize the rabbits if they didn't behave, and the rabbits decided to run away to a desert island. But the other animals, who lived at a great distance, shamed them, saying, 'You must stay where you are and be brave. This is no world for escapists. If the wolves attack you, we will come to your aid, in all probability.' So the rabbits continued to live near the wolves and one day there was a terrible flood which drowned a great many wolves. This was blamed on the rabbits, for it is well known that carrot-nibblers with long ears cause floods. The wolves descended on the rabbits, for their own good, and imprisoned them in a dark cave, for their own protection.

When nothing was heard about the rabbits for some weeks, the other animals demanded to know what had happened to them. The wolves replied that the rabbits had been eaten and since they had been eaten the affair was a purely internal matter. But the other animals warned that they might possibly unite against the wolves unless some reason was given for the destruction of the rabbits. So the wolves gave them one. 'They were trying to escape,' said the wolves, 'and, as you know, this is no world for escapists.'

Moral: Run, don't walk, to the nearest desert island.

James Thurber, *The Thurber Carnival* (1945)

pack number of animals that go about together **earthquake** sudden violent shaking of the earth's surface **to pound** strike heavily and repeatedly **hind** at the back **bolt** discharge (of lightning) **lettuce** ['letɪs] garden plant used in salads; G. Kopfsalat **desert** (adj.) barren, uninhabited **to shame** criticize, find fault with **escapist** s.o. who tries to get away from daily routine or reality **nibbler** s.o. eating in tiny bites **to descend (up)on** h. attack suddenly **internal** inner

3. The Zoo Story

CHARACTERS

PETER: A man in his early forties, neither fat nor gaunt, neither handsome nor homely. He wears tweeds, smokes a pipe, carries horn-rimmed glasses. Although he is moving into middle age, his dress and his manner would suggest a man younger.

JERRY: A man in his late thirties, not poorly dressed, but carelessly. What was once a trim and lightly muscled body has begun to go to fat; and while he is no longer handsome, it is evident that he once was. His fall from physical grace should not suggest debauchery; he has, to come closest to it, a great weariness.

It is Central Park; a Sunday afternoon in summer; the present. There are two park benches, one towards either side of the stage; they both face the audience. Behind them: foliage, trees, sky. At the beginning, PETER *is seated on one of the benches.*

[*As the curtain rises,* PETER *is seated on the bench stage-right. He is reading a book. He stops reading, cleans his glasses, goes back to reading.* JERRY *enters.*]

JERRY: I've been to the zoo. [PETER *doesn't notice.*] I said, I've been to the zoo. MISTER, I'VE BEEN TO THE ZOO!

PETER: Hm?... What?... I'm sorry, were you talking to me?

JERRY: I went to the zoo, and then I walked until I came here. Have I been walking north?

PETER [*puzzled*]: North? Why... I... I think so. Let me see.

JERRY [*pointing past the audience*]: Is that Fifth Avenue?

PETER: Why yes; yes, it is.

JERRY: And what is that cross street there; that one, to the right?

PETER: That? Oh, that's Seventy-fourth Street.

JERRY: And the zoo is around Sixty-fifth Street; so, I've been walking north.

PETER [*anxious to get back to his reading*]: Yes: it would seem so.

JERRY: Good old north.

PETER [*lightly, by reflex*]: Ha, ha.

JERRY [*after a slight pause*]: But not due north.

PETER: I... well, no, not due north; but, we... call it north. It's northerly.

Edward Albee (1959/60)

gaunt thin, as if ill or hungry **homely** plain **trim** fit; G. drahtig **evident** clear **debauchery** immoral behaviour **Central Park** large park in the centre of New York City **foliage** all the leaves of a tree or plant **stage-right** on the right side of the stage **puzzled** perplexed, confused **past** h. beyond **anxious** h. eager **due north** exactly, directly north

4. The Hangman at Home

What does the hangman think about
When he goes home at night from work?
When he sits down with his wife and
Children for a cup of coffee and a
Plate of ham and eggs, do they ask
Him if it was a good day's work
And everything went well or do they
Stay off some topics and talk about
The weather, baseball, politics
And the comic strips in the papers
And the movies? Do they look at his
Hands when he reaches for the coffee
Or the ham and eggs? If the little
Ones say, Daddy, play horse, here's

A rope-does he answer like a joke:
I seen enough rope for today?
Or does his face light up like a
Bonfire of joy and he does say:
It's a good and dandy world we live
In. And if a white face moon looks
In through a window where a baby girl
Sleeps and the moon-gleams mix with
Baby ears and baby hair-the hangman-
How does he act then? It must be easy
For him. Anything is easy for a hangman,
I guess.

Carl Sandburg (1878–1967)

to stay off avoid **rope** G. Seil, Strick **I seen** I have seen **bonfire** large fire made outdoors to celebrate some event **dandy** excellent, first-rate

5. Scotland

Aberdeen is the third biggest fishing port in Britain, having once been a very prosperous whaling port, before the invention of gas killed the market for whale-oil. When I was a boy about fifty years ago there was still a whaling station in use in the island of Harris in the Hebrides. The deep-sea fishermen have a world of their own, apart from ordinary men. They see their wives on average about once every seven days in the year. If you listen to the shipping forecast, you will hear intoned those evocative names, 'Iceland, Faeroes, Fair Isle, Bailey, Hebrides, Rockall', and picture the masthead lights rising and falling in the long cold seas.

A new frontier has been added to Scotland. A new element has come into our lives with the oil discoveries. Aberdeen harbour has been considerably enlarged and contains the most extraordinary-looking vessels, all to do with oilrigs. Every day twenty or thirty helicopters fly over the city headed for a hundred and some miles out to sea. There are now two American schools and one French school in Aberdeen for the use of the oil-drilling fraternity who come from those parts, and no one is in the least surprised to see men wearing a Stetson hat in any part of Aberdeen.

Some people tell us that we have reached a time when a millennium of perpetual prosperity is with us, arising from the oil. But we have a long history in Scotland, and we tend to be very sceptical of talk like this. We always say we will believe it when we see it.

Intensely wild as much of Scotland is, a great deal can be seen from the roads themselves. The Highland roads, with their passing places at intervals, call for a special technique of driving. You must judge whether you or the oncoming car is closer to the passing place, and whichever is the nearer draws in there. A fine code of politeness flowers from touching your hat to the other man if he has accommodated you in this way. Marshal Wade was sent to build roads in the Highlands so that armies could get in there and if necessary keep the clans in order. When the 1745 Rebellion came, the rebellious Highlanders used the good Marshal's roads for themselves to speed their march south. The difference between Highlands and Lowlands is one that you can feel immediately. It is a way of life and a separate people.

Lord Tweedsmuir, *The Country Life Picture Book of Scotland* (1977)

prosperous wealthy and successful **Hebrides** ['hebrɪdi:z] islands off the north-west coast of Scotland **evocative** [ɪ'vɒkətɪv] producing associations and feelings **masthead** top of a ship's mast **oil rig** construction for getting oil from beneath the sea **fraternity** group of people with the same work, interests, etc. **Stetson** cowboy hat **millennium of perpetual prosperity** future age of happiness and contentment

6. The Science to save us from Science

Since the beginning of the seventeenth century scientific discovery and invention have advanced at a continually increasing rate. This fact has made the last 350 years profoundly different from all previous ages. The gulf separating man from his past has widened from generation to generation, and finally from decade to decade. A reflective person, meditating on the extinction of trilobites, dinosaurs and mammoths, is driven to ask himself some very disquieting questions. Can our species endure so rapid a change? Can the habits which insured survival in a comparatively stable past still suffice amid the kaleidoscopic scenery of our time? And, if not, will it be possible to change ancient patterns of behaviour as quickly as the inventors change our material environment? No one knows the answer, but it is possible to survey probabilities, and to form some hypotheses as to the alternative directions that human development may take.

The first question is: Will scientific advance continue to grow more and more rapid, or will it reach a maximum speed and then begin to slow down?

The discovery of scientific method required genius, but its utilization requires only talent. An intelligent young scientist, if he gets a job giving access to a good laboratory, can be pretty certain of finding out something of interest, and may stumble upon some new fact of immense importance. Science, which was still a rebellious force in the early seventeenth century, is now integrated with the life of the community by the support of governments and universities. And as its importance becomes more evident, the number of people employed in scientific research continually increases. It would seem to follow that, so long as social and economic conditions do not become adverse, we may expect the rate of scientific advance to be maintained, and even increased, until some new limiting factor intervenes.

It might be suggested that, in time, the amount of knowledge needed before a new discovery could be made would become so great as to absorb all the best years of a scientist's life, so that by the time he reached the frontier of knowledge he would be senile. I suppose this may happen some day, but that day is certainly very distant. In the first place, methods of teaching improve. Plato thought that students in his academy would have to spend ten years learning what was then known of mathematics; nowadays any mathematically minded schoolboy learns much more mathematics in a year.

In the second place, with increasing specialization, it is possible to reach the frontier of knowledge along a narrow path, involving much less labour than a broad highway. In the third place, the frontier is not a circle but an irregular contour, in some places not far from the centre. Mendel's epoch-making discovery required little previous knowledge; what it needed was a life of elegant leisure spent in a garden. Radio-activity was discovered by the fact that some specimens of pitchblende were unexpectedly found to have photographed themselves in the dark. I do not think, therefore, that purely intellectual reasons will slow up scientific advances for a very long time to come.

There is another reason for expecting scientific advance to continue, and that is that it increasingly attracts the best brains. Leonardo da Vinci was equally pre-eminent in art and science, but it was from art that he derived his greatest fame. A man of similar endowments living at the present day would almost certainly hold some post which would require his giving all his time to science; if his politics were orthodox, he would probably be engaged in devising the hydrogen bomb, which our age would consider more useful than his pictures. The artist, alas, has not the status that he once had. Renaissance princes might compete for Michelangelo; modern states compete for nuclear physicists.

Bertrand Russell, in *The New York Times Magazine*, 19 March 1950

previous former **gulf** h. division **trilobite** ['traɪləbaɪt] extinct order of crustacea, whose remains are among the earliest known fossils **dinosaur** ['daɪnəsɔː] **species** ['spiːʃiːz] group having the same characteristics **insured** = ensured **to suffice** [sə'faɪs] be enough **kaleidoscopic** [kəlaɪdə'skɒpɪk] quickly changing **hypotheses** [haɪ'pɒθɪsiːz] (pl.) ideas put forward as a starting-point for reasoning **advance** progress **utilization** making use of **access to** h. right to use **to stumble upon** find unexpectedly **adverse** ['--] unfavourable **to intervene** come between in time; interfere **frontier** ['frʌntɪə] boundary; limit **senile** ['siːnaɪl] old and weak **mathematically minded** disposed to mathematics **contour** outline **Mendel** (1822–84) elaborated a theory of dominant and recessive characters governing heredity (G. Erbanlagen) **leisure** spare time **specimen** one of a class as an example **pitchblende** black mineral (oxide of uranium) yielding radium

7. I have a dream

(The following address was delivered in 1963 by Martin Luther King [1929–1968], a black Baptist minister, who led the mass civil rights movement in the U.S. from the mid–1950s. He won the Nobel Peace Prize in 1964. He was assassinated in 1968.)

I say to you today, my friends, even though we face the difficulties of today and tomorrow, I still have a dream. It is a dream deeply rooted in the American dream.

I have a dream that one day this nation will rise up and live out the true meaning of its creed: "We hold these truths to be self-evident; that all men are created equal."

I have a dream that one day on the red hills of Georgia the sons of former slaves and the sons of former slaveowners will be able to sit down together at the table of brotherhood.

I have a dream that one day even the state of Mississippi, a state sweltering with the heat of injustice, sweltering with the heat of oppression, will be transformed into an oasis of freedom and justice.

I have a dream that my four little children will one day live in a nation where they will not be judged by the color of their skin but by the content of their character.

I have a dream today.

I have a dream that one day down in Alabama with its vicious racists, with its governor having his lips dripping with the words of interposition and nullification, one day right there in Alabama little black boys and black girls will be able to join hands with little white boys and white girls as sisters and brothers.

I have a dream today.

I have a dream that one day every valley shall be exalted, every hill and mountain shall be made low, the rough places will be made plains, and the crooked places will be made straight, and the glory of the Lord shall be revealed, and all flesh shall see it together.

This is our hope. This is the faith that I go back to the South with. With this faith we will be able to hew out of the mountain of despair a stone of hope. With this faith we will be able to transform the jangling discords of our nation into a beautiful symphony of brotherhood. With this faith we will be able to work together, to pray together, to struggle together, to go to jail together, to stand up for freedom together, knowing that we will be free one day.

This will be the day when all of God's children will be able to sing with new meaning "My country 'tis of thee, sweet land of liberty, of thee I sing. Land where my fathers died, land of the pilgrim's pride, from every mountainside, let freedom ring."

And if America is to be a great nation this must become true. So let freedom ring from the prodigious hilltops of New Hampshire. Let freedom ring from the mighty mountains of New York. Let freedom ring from the heightening Alleghenies of Pennsylvania!

Let freedom ring from the snowcapped Rockies of Colorado!

Let freedom ring from the curvacious slopes of California!

But not only that; let freedom ring from Stone Mountain of Georgia!

Let freedom ring from Lookout Mountain of Tennessee.

Let freedom ring from every hill and mole hill of Mississippi.

From every mountainside, let freedom ring, and when this happens, when we allow freedom to ring, when we let it ring from every village and every hamlet, from every state and every city, we will be able to speed up that day when all of God's children, black men and white men, Jews and Gentiles, Protestants and Catholics, will be able to join hands and sing in the words of the old Negro spiritual, "Free at last! Free at last! Thank God almighty, we are free at last!"

to deliver h. give **to assassinate** kill (esp. an important politician) violently **rooted** h. firmly established **creed** (system of) beliefs or opinions **sweltering** sweating and suffering **vicious** very wicked, evil-minded **interposition and nullification** (U.S. law) the disputed doctrine that a state may refuse to recognize a Federal law **exalted** h. in high position **crooked** ['krʊkɪd] not level **to hew out** shape with force; G. herausmeißeln **jangling** harsh-soounding **prodigious** [prə'dɪdʒəs] huge **Alleghenies** ['ælɪgenɪz] mountain range in the eastern United States **curvacious** [kɜː'veɪʃəs] with shapely curves **mole hill** G. Maulwurfshügel **hamlet** small village **Gentiles** ['dʒentaɪlz] non-Jews

8. Beatable and Unbeatable

Children have a primitive but punctilious sense of what is fair and unfair. Two punishments for the same misdeed will not seem fair, especially if one consists of inconvenience and the other of physical pain. Punishment seen as unfair breeds mistrust of the system, not respect.

It is easy to appreciate the Government's dilemma. Eighteen months ago the European Court of Human Rights found against it in a case brought by Scottish parents who objected to the use of the tawse on their children. To implement that decision (which was concerned with parents' rights, not children's) only three courses were possible: to abandon corporal punishment in state schools; to make sure that parents everywhere were in reach of a state school where corporal punishment was banned; or to allow parents to opt out individually in schools that used the cane.

Britain is now the only country in Europe to sanction the use of the cane in its state schools. There is no compelling evidence that our children are naughtier than theirs. But many, perhaps most, parents and teachers still approve of the cane as a last resort punishment. The Government was therefore unwilling to ban it; and ensuring that all parents could find a school where it was not used was thought to be impossibly costly. So the Government fell back on parental discretion – a solution which the Scottish Lord Advocate rejected when putting the Government's case to the Court, on the excellent grounds that it was a fundamental principle that children in a school should be equally treated.

One other course was possible in theory – prevarication. States signing the European Convention on Human Rights undertake to abide by the Court's decisions in cases where they are parties. But the Court has no means of enforcing its decisions, and the sanction of expulsion from the Council of Europe (applied in the 1960s in the case of Greece) is in this context improbable. Only last week the Government made a mockery of a ruling of the other European Court in respect of EEC requirements on equal pay for women, when an Order which made only a token gesture towards implementation was moved by a junior minister under instructions to make plain by his demeanour the Government's contempt for this aspect of Britain's treaty obligations.

It is to Sir Keith Joseph's credit that he has taken no such ignominious course. The steady flow of similar cases heading towards the Court would have made the attempt most embarrassing to sustain. The plan proposed is unsatisfactory to all parties though it is brought forward in good faith as a workable solution. The alternative is to ensure at the earliest practicable time, that parents have within range a school that does not use corporal punishment. In areas where there is only one school, it will have to be that one.

The Times, 29 July 1983

punctilious very exact **inconvenience** discomfort or trouble **tawse** leather strap for punishing schoolchildren in Scotland **to abandon** give up completely **to sanction** authorize; allow **compelling** convincing **as a last resort** when all else has failed **to fall back on** turn to **discretion** [dɪsˈkreʃən] the freedom of choice **Lord Advocate** principal judge in Scotland **prevarication** the hiding of the truth **to abide by** keep (to) **expulsion** being thrown out **to make a mockery of** G. ad absurdum führen; verhöhnen **token** h. empty and meaningless **demeanour** way of behaving **ignominious** dishonourable **to sustain** keep up

9.

NO WONDER IT'S SO RELIABLE, THERE'S NOTHING TO GO WRONG.

Look what you get with the Citroën 2CV. A complete set of fully round wheels, one on each corner, for perfect mobility.

A peppy little engine tucked away up front, that not only starts with the turn of a key, but stops in exactly the same manner.

Completely transparent windows for superb all-round visibility.

A totally automated braking system, simply activated by depressing a pedal with the foot.

An automatic sunshine roof, you automatically roll it back when the sun comes out.

Central locking system. You can reach all the doors from the drivers seat, and many more features too numerous to mention.

In fact everything a driver will ever need to get him reliably and comfortably from A to B.

CITROËN 2CV £2499.

Price includes car tax, VAT and front seat belts, but excludes delivery and number plates. Citroën Cars Ltd., Mill Street, Slough SL2 5DE. Tel: Slough 23808. Check Yellow Pages for your nearest Citroën dealer.

reliable can be depended on **peppy** full of pep: lively **to tuck away** hide **transparent** can be seen through; G. durchsichtig **to depress** press down **feature** noticeable part or quality **VAT** value added tax; G. Mehrwertsteuer

10. Kicking the hospital habit

'The first thing the NHS needs is more money', you claim (*NS* 25 November). Nonsense; Britain spends less on its health services than other comparable countries for the good reason that doctors are not paid 'per item of service', which has escalated costs elsewhere – partly because of the temptation to prescribe unnecessary treatments, partly because of the army of administrators, insurance employees and so on.

What is needed is saner distribution of the NHS's present income. As things are, nearly two thirds of it goes to hospitals, because the consultants who run the show work and teach in hospitals. Most of the patients now in hospital would not be there if the health services had been designed to keep people out of them; but so long as the medical profession retains its monopolistic position, there is no prospect of switching resources to preventive medicine, or of bringing in those alternative practitioners who are now helping more and more people to avoid the dire consequences of orthodoxy's drug-dependence.

Brian Inglis, London NW3, *New Statesman*, 9 December 1983

to kick the habit (coll.) stop a regular activity **NHS** National Health Service **comparable** ['kɒmpərəbl] **per item of service** for every aspect of treatment **to escalate** cause to increase rapidly **to prescribe** order the use of **sane** h. reasonable **to run the show** (coll.) control the business or organization **to retain** keep; continue to have or hold **preventive** serving to hinder; G. vorbeugend **dire** terrible **orthodoxy** generally accepted opinions or practice **drug-dependence** excessive prescription of medicine **Inglis** ['ɪŋəls]

11. The Glass Menagerie

The Glass Menagerie is set in the thirties, when America was in the throes of the Depression and labour disturbances were to be found in many, perhaps most, cities. Williams' narrator, Tom Wingfield, calls it 'a memory play… sentimental… not realistic', and this surely is true, in its way, but the saga of Tom, Laura and Amanda Wingfield *is* in many ways realistic, with Tom, who displays so many characteristics of Williams himself – poet, free spirit, one of the playwright's 'fugitive kind'. Like Williams, as noted earlier, Tom is an employee in a shoe factory. Amanda, Tom's mother, deserted by her husband, surely has her genesis in the playwright's own mother, one of the once gracious ladies of the now impoverished South, and it is not improbable to suggest that his sister Laura, shy, sensitive, insecure, coming to life almost entirely in terms of her 'glass menagerie' (a collection of glass animals), was inspired by Williams' sister Rose, whose withdrawal from everyday life culminated in a lifelong institutionalization.

It is Laura, victim of a minor physical disability, victim, also, of the world's expectations and demands, who provides the play's focus. She is 'terribly shy', has dropped out of business college after only a few days, a fact unknown to her mother, who fears the twenty-three-year-old girl will become an old maid. She 'lives in a world of her own'. Amanda becomes obsessed with the idea of getting her a 'gentleman caller'. It is an idea that begins to take possession of the Wingfields' apartment and it comes to a form of fruition when Tom, trapped and frustrated in his job at the Continental Shoemakers' warehouse, brings home a more ambitious fellow worker, Jim, 'an emissary from a world of reality that we were somehow set apart from'. For Amanda has suggested to Tom one of Williams' recurring themes, the inroads of time: 'You are the only young man that I know of who ignores the fact that the future becomes the present, the present the past and the past turns into everlasting regret if you don't plan for it!'

Jim's appearance transforms Laura. They had been high school classmates and she had fallen in love with him, though he seems oblivious to her existence. She reveals 'a fragile, unearthly prettiness... like a piece of translucent glass touched by light, given a momentary radiance, not actual, not lasting'.

Catherine Hughes, *American Playwrights 1945–75* (1976)

in the throes of struggling with **labour disturbance** strike action **saga** [sɑːgə] family chronicle **to display** show **fugitive** running away, escaping **to desert** leave **genesis** origin **gracious** h. polite, elegant and well-to-do **impoverished** made poor **in terms of** in the context of **withdrawal** moving away **to culminate** reach the highest point **institutionalization** being kept in a mental hospital **victim of** h. suffering from **disability** handicap **focus** centre of interest **to be obsessed** have a fixed idea **caller** h. visitor **fruition** fulfilment **trapped** caught **emissary** ['emɪsərɪ] messenger **recurring** repeated **inroads** effects **oblivious to** unaware of **fragile** ['frædʒaɪl] easily injured, broken or hurt **translucent** allowing light to pass through **radiance** brightness

12. The Impact of Energy on Geological Processes

Geology is a science of matter and energy. The matter in this case is the earth. The earth is an astronomical body – a planet – which comprises three distinct material aggregates: an atmospheric envelope, which is gaseous; an aqueous semi-envelope in the form of the liquid oceans; and finally the earth's principal mass, which is solid. A part of the matter on the earth's surface is aggregated into the organic forms, plants and animals – the only organisms so far known in the universe.

The energy manifestations on the earth are represented by the kinetic and potential energy of its planetary motions, by the input and outward reradiation of solar energy, and by the heat escaping from the earth's interior. As a result of these fluxes of energy, the matter in the earth's surface environment is maintained in a state of continuous or intermittent circulation. Winds blow; ocean waves, currents and tides are formed; water is evaporated and falls as rain or snow; rivers flow; and plants and animals grow, reproduce themselves, and die. Less continuous, or much slower, manifestations of terrestrial energy are the sudden jolts of earthquakes, the eruption of volcanoes, and the slow erection and erosional destruction of mountain ranges.

The earth's gravitational field is the combined result of the attraction upon a unit mass at any given point of all the separate masses of the earth and the centrifugal force due to the earth's rotation. This field determines the shape of the sea-level surface of the earth, since the surface of a body of water at rest is perpendicular at each point to the direction of gravity. The precise determination of the shape and size of the earth, which is the principal object of the subscience of geodesy, is thus very intimately concerned with the mapping of the earth's gravitational field, not only locally on land but over the whole earth. From the shape and size of the earth, and the value of gravity, it is possible to determine the mass of the earth. Then the ratio of the earth's mass to its volume gives the mean density of its materials.

The earth's atmosphere and its oceans, its running streams and the circulation of its water beneath the ground are all manifestations of the mechanics and thermodynamics of fluids. The particular studies of the atmosphere, the oceans, and of the water circulation of the earth comprise, respectively, the subsciences of meteorology, oceanography, and of hydrology.

One of the most important facts about running water is that it is continuously eroding the land and transporting the products in the form of sands and muds in streams and dumping them into the ocean. We are thus led to wonder how long it will be until there will be no land left above the level of the sea.

M. King Hubbert (1965)

to comprise include **aggregate** ['ægrɪgət] composition of mass **gaseous** [geɪsjəs] G. gasartig **aqueous** [eɪkwɪəs] watery **to aggregate** ['ægrɪgeɪt] compose, bring together **kinetic** concerning motion **potential** present but inactive **solar** ['səʊlə] of the sun **flux** continuous change **intermittent** pausing from time to time **tides** rise and fall of sea-level **to evaporate** convert a liquid into a gas **terrestrial** of the earth **jolt** shake **eruption** outbreak **erection** building up **erosional** concerning the process of being worn away or eroded **range** line **perpendicular** at right angles **subscience** branch of a science **geodesy** [dʒɪ'ɒdɪsɪ] measuring and mapping out the curved surface of the earth **ratio** ['reɪʃɪəʊ] relation between two amounts expressed by dividing one by the other, e.g. 1 : 16 **mean** h. arithmetical average **density** G. Dichte **thermodynamics** ['θɜːməʊdaɪ'næmɪks] processes involving heat changes and the conversion of energy **fluid** substance which takes the shape of its container, e.g. a liquid or a gas, but not a solid **hydrology** [haɪ'drɒlədʒɪ] study of water in the hydrosphere, i.e. oceans, seas, etc., and in the atmosphere **to dump** deposit

13. Decision to give parents choice on the cane criticized as unworkable

Parents are to be allowed to exempt their children from corporal punishment in schools, but the cane will not be abolished, it was announced yesterday.

The Government's decision means that two forms of descipline will operate within the same school and some teachers fear that that will create big problems.

The plan was criticized by the National Union of Teachers, the largest teachers' union, which has 250,000 members. Mr. Douglas McAvoy, its deputy general secretary, said that it would create chaos.

"It is part of the Government's privatization plan. We can envisage the mass sale of 'I Cannot Be Beaten' badges".

Mr. Tom Scott, of the Society of Teachers Opposed to Physical Punishment, said that the policy would be unworkable. His organization would urge parents to exempt their children.

Mr. Scott said he would complain to Strasbourg, "in view of the deliberate defiance of the British Government of the European Court ruling which had already been delayed for 18 months".

Mr. Peter Dawson, general secretary of the Professional Association of Teachers, which has 23,000 members said: "It is unthinkable to have two different disciplinary systems operating in one school".

The new policy is designed to meet last year's judgment by the European Court of Human Rights which said that children should not be beaten against their parents' philosophical convictions.

A document published yesterday by the Department of Education and Science, to coincide with a parliamentary question to Sir Keith

Joseph, the Secretary of State for Education and Science, says that there will be consultations on implementation, but not about the decision.

Sir Keith said in a Commons written reply that he believed parents would exercise their right to opt out "responsibly". "We are concerned to allow schools the maximum freedom, consistent with such a right of exemption, to employ for the maintenance of discipline such sanctions, including corporal punishment, as they judge to be appropriate".

The abolition of corporal punishment in England and Wales is ruled out on the ground that many parents and teachers favour its retention.

The department said yesterday that it had conducted no new public opinion poll but that its impression was that most parents favoured the cane.

The document rules out setting up corporal punishment and non corporal punishment schools as being expensive, impractical and administratively cumbersome.

It outlines three ways in which parents could opt out of corporal punishment for their children: leaving the initiative to parents who opposed it; leaving the initiative to those who do not object; or asking parents to state their preference. The document says the third approach would give the clearest picture, but involve the most work.

The document is being sent to local authority, teacher, and parent associations for comments, which should be made before the end of November. Legislation is not envisaged until 1984.

Lucy Hodges, *The Times*, 29 July 1983

cane wooden stick for punishing schoolchildren **to exempt** free from **corporal** bodily **to abolish** put an end to **deputy** (adj.) second-in-charge; G. stellvertretend **to envisage** see as a future possibility **badge** G. Abzeichen **to urge** strongly recommend **deliberate** intentional **defiance** [dɪ'faiəns] open disrespect for and/or opposition to **to meet** h. satisfy **to coincide with**[ˌkəʊɪn'saɪd] happen at the same time **implementation** carrying out **Commons written reply** a written answer to the House of Commons by a government minister **to opt out** choose not to take part **consistent with** in agreement with **maintenance** ['meɪntənəns] h. the keeping up of **sanction** h. punishment **retention** continued existence **to conduct a public opinion poll** ask a representative group of people about their opinions on a certain subject **cumbersome** difficult to deal with **preference** ['prefərəns]

14. Precautions

- Before trying to operate the unit, make sure that Timer Rec Switch is OFF.
- Take special care not to use or store the unit for a long period of time in direct sunlight, in excessively hot, cold, damp or dusty places, or places subject to heavy vibrations.
- If the unit is suddenly moved from a cold place to a warm place, moisture that can cause damage to both the tape and the unit may form inside the unit. Avoid such changes in temperature, if possible. When excessive moisture is present inside the unit, the Moisture Indicator Lamp will light up and the unit shuts off automatically to prevent damage to the tape or the video recording mechanism.
- Avoid operating or storing the unit and the video cassette near appliances generating strong magnetic fields (large motors, power transformers, or large audio speakers).

- Do not block or cover the ventilation slots on top, back and bottom of the unit. Especially avoid soft materials such as cloth or paper.
- Use the unit in horizontal position and do not place anything heavy on the unit.
- Keep the unit away from flower vases, tub, sink, etc. If liquids should be spilled into the unit, serious damage will be caused. If you spill any liquid into the unit consult qualified service personnel.
- Do not insert fingers or any other objects into the cassette holder.
- Do not spray any cleaner or wax directly on the unit or use forced air to remove dust.

Video Cassette Recorder Operating Instructions (1984)

precaution care taken to keep away from danger **to operate** use **unit** apparatus; system **to store** keep **damp** slightly wet **subject to** exposed to **moisture** dampness **damage** harm **indicator** h. G. Kontroll- **appliance** [ə'plaɪəns] instrument **power transformer** G. Netzteil **audio speaker** loudspeaker **slot** narrow opening **tub** bath **sink** large basin, esp. in a kitchen **liquid** substance like water or oil **to spill** pour out without wanting to **to consult** ask advice from s.o. **personnel** [ˌpɜːsə'nel] people employed by a company **to insert** put in **forced air** compressed air

15.

An Agreement made

the 4th **day of** September

One Thousand Nine Hundred and 79

BETWEEN

ROSANNE JARRETT

of WELL COTTAGE, CHARMINSTER, DORCHESTER

(hereinafter called "the Landlord" which expression shall where the context admits include the person for the time being entitled to the reversion immediately expectant on the determination of the tenancy hereby created) of the one part and

of REINHARD KEMNITZ

(hereinafter called "the Tenant" which expression shall where the context admits include his successors in title) of the other part

Whereby **it is agreed as follows:—**

1. THE Landlord lets and the Tenant takes ALL THAT [messuage or dwelling-house with the appurtenances thereto belonging] [*or* flat] situate at and known as

20 EAST HILL, CHARMINSTER, DORCHESTER.

(hereinafter called "the premises")

Together with the Fixtures and Fittings set forth in the [first] Schedule hereto [and the use of the entrance hall and lift (if any) staircase vestibule and outer door of the said building in common with the other tenants and occupiers of the premises] (*see Note* 4) [and the Furniture and Effects in the said premises (as the same are more particularly described in the [second] Schedule hereto)] (*see Note* 3)

TO HOLD the same unto the Tenant for the term of **commencing on the** 4th **day of** September **19** 79 **[and terminating on the** 31st **day of** July **19** 80 **] [*or* and thereafter from** **to** **until the tenancy hereby created shall be determined by either party giving to the other at least** one month's **notice in writing to quit expiring at the end of the first or any subsequent** **thereafter].**

AT the Rent of £ 24 **for every** week **of the said term to be payable in advance without any deduction whatsoever on the days and by the instalments following that is to say**

the first of such payments to be made on the 4th **day of** September **19** 79 **next.**

hereinafter from now on **to admit** h. allow **to be entitled to** have a right to **reversion** right to possess property in certain circumstances **expectant on** h. G. gültig bei **determination of the tenancy** signing of a contract giving the right to use a house etc. for a certain period **successor** person who comes next **title** h. place and rights **messuage** ['mesjʊɪdʒ] G. Anwesen **appurtenance** right connected with the renting of a house **premises** house or building with its outbuildings, land, etc. **fixture** s.th. fixed in place, esp. built-in cupboards, electric light fittings, sanitary installations, etc. **fitting** h. furnishing **schedule** h. list **vestibule** lobby or entrance hall to a building **occupier** person in temporary possession of land or a building **effects** goods, property **unto** (obs.) to **to commence** begin **to terminate** come to an end **notice** a formal warning of intention to end an agreement or contract at a certain time **to quit** leave **to expire** come to an end **subsequent** ['sʌbsɪkwənt] following **deduction** h. G. Abzug **instalment** sum of money to be paid at regular times over a specified period

Chapter II

Text – Structure and Types

Introductory Remarks

The structure of a text is determined by the principles of composition and the use of text types. In other words, text forms are analysed in order to find out the logical structure in a text and the interrelation between text sections. The purpose of this analysis is to pinpoint the interrelation between form, content, internal composition, and textual/authorial intention.

Initially, there are three main sections to a text: the introductory, the middle, and the final sections. These three sections are linked together, and therefore a certain coherence or interrelation between the sections is established. It should be noticed, however, that for the structure of a text only the middle section is indispensable.

The introductory section (introduction, exposition) usually consists of elements leading up to the main section of the respective text form. Generally, the essential functions of an introduction may be described as follows: the initial situation is described in preparation for the main section; facts and prior events are narrated; themes and characters are introduced; a theory or theories is/are put forward. The term exposition is reserved for the introductory part(s) of fictional texts. The exposition presents the initial setting, action and events, and characters (when, where, who, what).

The middle section of a text is composite in character, normally made up of a number of text units presenting the description, reflection, action or argumentation essential to the text as a whole. Depending on the text form, the middle section can serve its main purpose as an extension and progression of the text's subject matter by a narration and illustration of events, the detailed study of characters, the demonstration and discussion of theories, and so on. Generally, this section of a text serves as the basis of a text and forms the build-up to the conclusions in the final section.

The final section contains the evaluation of a text's preceding ideas, action, and/or description. The summary may take the form of a sudden appeal, a(n) (in)conclusive evaluation, a(n) (anti-)climactic rounding off of plot, or even unresolved conflicts or 'unfinished' plots.

As regards the internal composition of a text, many varieties of structuring can be identified, e.g. the chronological, the antithetical, the enumerative, the symmetrical, the parallel. Other fundamental patterns of structuring are the development from the general to the particular and back to the general; the causal relation – cause to effect and/or the reverse; the (anti-)climactic build-up to the conclusion.

The intention of text study can also be the study of the use of different text types. Text types constitute the formal basis of text forms; the intention of a text form considerably influences the choice of text types, e.g. instruction manuals make particular use of the instructive text type. These text types are also governed by the compositional principle of an internal logic, which distinguishes between the expository approach, the descriptive and narrative approaches, the argumentative and instructive approaches, with or without a final climax. The following text types are generally accepted as covering all text forms. The definitions are simplified explanations of these theoretical concepts:

– descriptive text:	makes statement(s) about the physical and outer appearances of people, things, and situations and/or their spatial arrangement. A description can be either a neutral observation or a more personal and subjective one.
– narrative text:	makes statement(s) about the action that takes place in a text. These actions and events constitute the plot.
– expository text:	sets out to relate concepts, ideas, or opinions in a step-by-step or analytical fashion. This text can be either neutral or subjective.
– argumentative text:	discusses a number of conflicting standpoints in an attempt to evaluate the relationship between these different ideas. This evaluation takes the form of a conclusion.
– instructive text:	aims to give systematic directions on usage, action, or behaviour.

Several text types may be found within one text; however, one text type will normally predominate, the choice depending largely on the intention of a particular text form such as information, manipulation, imagination.

spatial arrangement G. räumliche Anordnung

1. Give a short summary/plot outline of each text.
2. Point out the structure of the text
   – by dividing it into its main sections
   – by analysing the function of each part
   – by examining the composition of these text sections and their interrelation.
3. Identify the text type(s) in the text. If there is more than one decide which text type is the predominant one. Give reasons.
4. Creative writing: compose your own text, basing it on one of the five text types.

Points for discussion:

arrogance, love, progress vs. conservatism, patriotism, the family.

Useful Phrases

1. To	reveal	the	composition	of the text
	uncover		structure	
	disclose			
	analyse			

2. The text is	arranged	according to a certain pattern
	organised	
	structured	

3. The text	is divided into	three	paragraphs
	is composed of		parts
	contains		sections
			sequences

4. The text is entitled…

5. The first	part	constitutes the introduction
	paragraph	

6. The introduction	sets forth the problem in question
	presents the principal ideas
	enumerates the points to be developed

7. The starting point of an argumentation

8. The	problem	is	presented	in a step-by-step fashion
	situation		analysed	
	theme			

9. The text	deals with	different aspects of a problem
	presents	
	sets forth	

10. The	line of argumentation
	train of thought
	sequence of ideas

11. The author	puts forward presents develops	a thesis

12. In the main section the author	passes from… to… takes up another subject returns to

13. The author	digresses from the main topic varies the theme changes the topic	by alluding to

14. To stick to a subject
To continue with the same subject

15. The author	plays off balances	ideas against one another

16. To support an argument with the help of	an example a comparison a contrast

17. to develop	a thought conception standpoint an idea opinion

18. The	final section conclusion	consists of comprises	a	comment summary

19. The text	concludes finishes closes	with

20. to arrange s.th. in a(n)	climactic anti-climactic	order

1. The Scotty Who Knew Too Much

Several summers ago there was a Scotty who went to the country for a visit. He decided that all the farm dogs were cowards, because they were afraid of a certain animal that had a white stripe down its back. 'You are a pussy-cat and I can lick you,' the Scotty said to the farm dog who lived in the house where the Scotty was visiting. 'I can lick the little animal with the white stripe, too. Show him to me.' 'Don't you want to ask any questions about him?' said the farm dog. 'Naw,' said the Scotty. '*You* ask the questions.'

So the farm dog took the Scotty into the woods and showed him the white-striped animal and the Scotty closed in on him, growling and slashing. It was all over in a moment and the Scotty lay on his back.

When he came to, the farm dog said, 'What happened?' 'He threw vitriol,' said the Scotty, 'but he never laid a glove on me.'

A few days later the farm dog told the Scotty there was another animal all the farm dogs were afraid of. 'Lead me to him,' said the Scotty. 'I can lick anything that doesn't wear horseshoes.' 'Don't you want to ask any questions about him?' said the farm dog. 'Naw', said the Scotty. 'Just show me where he hangs out.' So the farm dog led him to a place in the woods and pointed out the little animal when he came along. 'A clown,' said the Scotty, 'a pushover,' and he closed in, leading with his left and exhibiting some mighty fancy footwork. In less than a second the Scotty was flat on his back, and when he woke up the farm dog was pulling quills out of him. 'What happened?' said the farm dog. 'He pulled a knife on me,' said the Scotty, 'but at least I have learned how you fight out here in the country, and now I am going to beat *you* up.' So he closed in on the farm dog, holding his nose with one front paw to ward off the vitriol and covered his eyes with the other front paw to keep out the knives. The Scotty couldn't see his opponent and he couldn't smell his opponent and he was so badly beaten that he had to be taken back to the city and put in a nursing home.

Moral: It is better to ask some of the questions than to know all the answers.

James Thurber, *The Thurber Carnival* (1945)

Scotty a Scotch terrier **coward** person who runs away from danger **to lick** h. (coll.) overcome; triumph over **naw** no **to close in on s.o.** come nearer in order to attack **to growl** make a low threatening sound **to slash** h. make striking movements **vitriol** ['vɪtrɪəl] G. ätzende Flüssigkeit **to lay a glove on s.o.** (coll.) hit, strike **pushover** person who is easily overcome or controlled **to lead with o.'s left** G. links auslegen (beim Boxen) **to exhibit** show **mighty fancy footwork** (coll.) very skilful movements of legs and feet **quill** long sharp stiff spike of a porcupine; G. Stachel **to ward off** keep away; avoid **opponent** person against whom one fights **nursing home** small private hospital

2. Early Autumn

When Bill was very young, they had been in love. Many nights they had spent walking, talking together. Then something not very important had come between them, and they didn't speak. Impulsively, she had married a man she thought she loved. Bill went away, bitter about women.

Yesterday, walking across Washington Square, she saw him for the first time in years.

"Bill Walker," she said.

He stopped. At first he did not recognize her, to him she looked so old.

"Mary! Where did you come from?"

Unconsciously, she lifted her face as though wanting a kiss, but he held out his hand. She took it.

"I live in New York now," she said.

"Oh" – smiling politely. Then a little frown came quickly between his eyes.

"Always wondered what happened to you, Bill."

"I'm a lawyer. Nice firm, way downtown."

"Married yet?"

"Sure. Two kids."

"Oh," she said.

A great many people went past them through the park.

People they didn't know. It was late afternoon. Nearly sunset. Cold.

"And your husband?" he asked her.

"We have three children. I work in the bursar's office at Columbia."

"You're looking very..." (he wanted to say *old*) "... well," he said.

She understood. Under the trees in Washington Square, she found herself desperately reaching back into the past. She had been older than he then in Ohio. Now she was not young at all. Bill was still young.

"We live on Central Park West," she said. "Come and see us sometime."

"Sure," he replied. "You and your husband must have dinner with my family some night. Any night. Lucille and I'd love to have you."

The leaves fell slowly from the trees in the Square. Fell without wind. Autumn dusk. She felt a little sick.

"We'd love it," she answered.

"You ought to see my kids." He grinned.

Suddenly the lights came on up the whole length of Fifth Avenue, chains of misty brilliance in the blue air.

"There's my bus," she said.

He held out his hand, "Good-bye."

"When..." she wanted to say, but the bus was ready to pull off. The lights on the avenue blurred, twinkled, blurred.

And she was afraid to open her mouth as she entered the bus. Afraid it would be impossible to utter a word.

Suddenly she shrieked very loudly, "Good-bye!" But the bus door had closed.

The bus started. People came between them outside, people crossing the street, people they didn't know. Space and people. She lost sight of

Bill. Then she remembered she had forgotten to give him her address – or to ask him for his – or tell him that her youngest boy was named Bill, too.

Langston Hughes (1963)

Washington Square park in Greenwich Village, New York where all kinds of people meet **unconsciously** (adv.) unaware, without realizing **frown** the drawing together of the eyebrows, causing lines on the forehead **lawyer** G. Rechtsanwalt **way downtown** normally refers to the business centre of a city; h. probably around Wall Street **kid** (coll.) child **bursar** [ˈbɜːsə] G. Schatzmeister, Quästor **Columbia** i.e. Columbia University, large private university of the Ivy League, on the Upper West Side of Manhattan **Central Park West** a cosmopolitan living area west of Central Park, New York's largest and best-known public park situated in the heart of Manhattan **dusk** time just before it gets dark **Fifth Ave.** Fifth Avenue, famous shopping street in Manhattan **misty** not clear **to pull off** start to leave **to blur** be unclear, indistinct **to twinkle** be unsteady **to shriek** scream, cry out loud

3. How can she be happy

How can she be happy
when the man she loves is unhappy

He feels she is blackmailing him
by making him feel guilty
because she is unhappy that he is unhappy

She feels he is trying to destroy her love for him
by accusing her of being selfish
when the trouble is
that she can't be so selfish as to be happy
when the man she loves is unhappy

She feels that there must be something wrong with her
to love someone who can be so cruel
as to destroy her love for him
and is too guilty to be happy, and is unhappy because
he is guilty

He feels that he is unhappy because he is guilty
to be happy when others are unhappy and that he made
a mistake to marry someone who can only think of
happiness

R. D. Laing

to blackmail force s.o. to do s.th. against his will **guilty** having done wrong **to accuse s.o. of doing s.th.** say that s.o. has done wrong **selfish** chiefly interested in and thinking of one's own needs and welfare

4. Vintage Stuff

The arrival of Peregrine Roderick Clyde-Browne on earth was authenticated by his birth certificate. His father was named as Oscar Motley Clyde-Browne, occupation Solicitor, and his mother as Marguerite Diana, maiden name Churley. Their address was The Cones, Pinetree Lane, Virginia Water. It was also announced in *The Times* with the additional note, 'Most grateful thanks to the staff of St. Barnabas' Nursing Home.'

The thanks were premature but at the time sincere. Mr. and Mrs. Clyde-Browne had waited a long time for a child and were about to resort to medical help when Peregrine was conceived. Mrs. Clyde-Browne was then thirty-six and her husband already forty. They were therefore understandably delighted when, after a surprisingly easy labour, Peregrine weighed in at 8 lb 5 oz at 6 a.m. on 25 March 196-.

'He's a beautiful baby,' said the Sister with greater regard for Mrs. Clyde-Browne's feelings than for the facts. Peregrine's beauty was of the sort usually seen after a particularly nasty car accident. 'And such a good one.'

Here she was nearer the truth. From the moment of his birth Peregrine was good. He seldom cried, ate regularly and had just the right amount of wind to reassure his parents that he was thoroughly normal. In short, for the first five years he was a model child and it was only when he continued to be a model child through his sixth, seventh, eighth and ninth years that the Clyde-Brownes had cause to wonder if Peregrine was more model than was entirely proper for a small boy.

'Behaviour: Impeccable?' said Mr. Clyde-Browne, reading his school report. Peregrine went to a very expensive preparatory school as a day-boy. 'I find that a little disturbing.'

'I can't imagine why. Peregrine has always been a very good boy and I think it does us credit as his parents.'

'I suppose so, though when I was his age nobody said my behaviour was impeccable. On the contrary...'

'You were an extremely naughty little boy. Your mother admitted as much.'

'My mother would,' said Mr. Clyde-Browne, whose feelings for his late mother were mixed. 'And I don't much like this "Tries hard" against all the subjects. I'd rather his work was impeccable and his behaviour left something to be desired.'

'Well, you can't have everything. If he misbehaved you'd call him a hooligan or vandal or something. Be grateful he tries hard at work and doesn't get into trouble.'

So for the time being Mr. Clyde-Browne left it at that and Peregrine continued to be a model child. It was only after another year of impeccable behaviour and hard trying that Mr. Clyde-Browne approached the headmaster for a fuller report on his son.

Tom Sharpe (1983)

to authenticate verify, prove **occupation** profession **solicitor** G. Notar und Rechtsanwalt **maiden name** family name of a woman before marriage **staff** group of persons working under the same management **nursing home** small private hospital **premature** ['premətjʊə] before the usual or proper time; too early **sincere** genuine and honest **to resort to** turn to (for help) **to conceive** [kən'si:v] h. become pregnant **labour** process of childbirth; G. Wehen **8 lb 5 oz** 8 pounds and 5 ounces; 1 ounce = 28.35 grams; 1 pound = 454 grams **regard** concern, consideration **wind** the passing of wind noisily out of the mouth from the stomach **to reassure** remove the fears and doubts **impeccable** faultless **preparatory school** [prɪ'pærətərɪ] private school where pupils are prepared for entry to a secondary private school **day-boy** boy who attends (a private) school during the day but sleeps at home **to do s.o. credit** be a cause of honour and satisfaction **to admit** acknowledge **late** dead **against** beside (written on a school report) **hooligan** rowdy **vandal** person who intentionally damages or destroys things

5. New Lamps for Old

In this age when every argument is dominated by the economic factor, when happiness is equated with material prosperity and when bigger is always better, it is not easy to make a case for any sort of conservation...

It is really a hopeless task to try to suggest a middle course between the 'stop everything from happening' lot on the one hand and the 'all change is inevitably for the better' enthusiasts on the other.

The fact remains, however, that once you get out of the hothouse atmosphere of the 'avante-garde' and the 'precious preserves', there is a very broad band of opinion which can see both the value of what has gone before and the practical advantages of the new. This apparent contradiction is really nothing more than good old-fashioned compromise which, over the centuries, has succeeded in making life tolerable for vast numbers of people...

No-one in their senses would deny the need for efficient industrial, commercial and agricultural buildings, but it is also quite reasonable to expect developers, planners, architects and owners to use a bare minimum of consideration and good taste, though one can be forgiven for wondering if some of them have heard of that expression.

There is a considerable body of opinion, misguided though it may be, which feels that efficiency and commercial success is only one of the factors which should be allowed to influence the human environment. It holds that there are other, perhaps less tangible, factors which should also be permitted to exert some influence. Ordinary pleasure, daily satisfaction, the stimulation of the senses, the atmosphere created by brilliant design; these are all things which convert material prosperity into what is known as civilisation. After all, it hardly matters what level of prosperity is reached if the human spirit cannot flourish. A successful space flight is hardly adequate compensation for concentration camps and the suppression of critical comment.

H. R. H. The Duke of Edinburgh

to equate with regard as being equal **prosperity** wealth or success **to make a case for** support **lot** (coll.) group of people **inevitable** [ɪn'evɪtəbl] always; without exception **hothouse** active and powerful; highly charged with emotion **avante-garde** the modern and progressive **precious preserves** the highly regarded conservative attitudes **apparent** seeming **no one in their senses** no sensible person **to deny** [dɪ'naɪ] refuse to accept or believe **consideration** common sense; thought **body of opinion** number of people sharing the same opinion **to misguide** confuse; mislead **to hold** claim **tangible** clear; obvious **to permit** allow **to exert** exercise; use **to convert** change; transform **to flourish** develop and do well **adequate** [ædɪkwət] satisfactory **suppression** official banning **H.R.H.** His Royal Highness

6. Proud to be British

What social surveys tell us about patriotism today

This week's celebration of the fortieth anniversary of D-day is a pointed reminder of how ideas about patriotism change. Nearly every Briton who lived through those days is proud of the contribution that the country made to the defeat of Hitler. Yet today, many people feel uneasy when politicians evoke patriotic emotions to justify the threat of force.

The patriotic rhetoric of Shakespeare no longer reflects the sentiments of the intellectuals and writers of England, a tribe *sans patrie*. Rupert Brooke's hymn to "some corner of a foreign field" that is made "for ever England" by the body of a dead soldier, is rejected as deluded or dangerous. When the subject of patriotism is mentioned, it is in Dr. Johnson's sense: "Patriotism is the last refuge of a scoundrel."

But what do ordinary British people think about their country? Do the sentiments of left-wing playwrights or of right-wing newspaper proprietors more nearly reflect their views? Since patriotism is a fundamental political value, it was included in a major international survey originated by the European Value System Study Group, and conducted in Britain by the Gallup Poll. The survey has covered more than a dozen countries, including the United States and Japan. The values survey adopted a very straightforward approach to the measurement of patriotic sentiment, asking each respondent: How proud are you to be British? Avoiding abstract theoretical terms reduced the proportion of Don't Knows to 3 per cent.

Patriotism is a value that unites the British people; 86 per cent say that they are proud to be British. They differ only in the strength of their pride. An absolute majority, 55 per cent, give three cheers: they are very proud to be British. Another 31 per cent give two cheers: they are quite proud to be British. By contrast, only 8 per cent say that they are not very proud to be British, and only 3 per cent that they are not at all proud.

Richard Rose, *New Society*, 7 June 1984

survey h. questioning of public opinion **anniversary** yearly return of the date of an event **D-day** (D for unnamed day) major allied invasion in Northern France on 6 June 1944 **pointed** striking **reminder** s.th. to make one remember **contribution** h. active support or help **to evoke** create **to justify** show to be right, reasonable or proper **rhetoric** ['retərik] G. Redekunst **sentiment** feeling or emotion **tribe** (often uncivilised) racial group with its own beliefs, culture, customs and language; G. Volksstamm **sans patrie** without a mother country **Rupert Brooke** English poet (1887–1915), known for his patriotic poems **deluded** mistaken **Dr. Johnson** English critic and poet (1709–1784) **refuge** ['refju:dʒ] place which gives protection or shelter from danger **scoundrel** evil person **playwright** writer of plays **proprietor** owner **to conduct** carry out **Gallup Poll** a questioning of people's opinions, carried out by the Gallup Institute **to adopt** take and use **approach to s.th.** method of doing s.th. **respondent** person questioned **to give three cheers** agree completely and enthusiastically with

7. Real Kids vs. 'The Average' Family

These days there is no shortage of people – that is, adult people – who are prepared to share their worries about changes in the American family. Pediatricians and child psychologists meeting in Philadelphia two years ago summarized the general mood with their conference title: "The Family – Can It Be Saved?" A year and a half hence, the theme will be pondered at a major White House Conference on the Family. Between now and then, we should hear a word from the children growing up in the changing American family, who have their own concerns or worries about the trend.

Consider eight-year-old Susan. After a month of second grade in a suburban school, she told her mother that she felt "funny" because there were no other children like her in the class, children from single-parent homes. Yet when mother and daughter reviewed Susan's class list together, they found that 21 of the 33 children came from single-parent families.

Susan's sense of difference – of not quite fitting – is one shared by many young children today. The reality around them has changed, but the myths they learn from still tell them an older story. While our educational system and mass media, by and large, go on depicting the "average American family" as the two-parent family – with Daddy hard at work and Mommy at home taking care of the children – significant numbers of children are growing up in families of very different composition.

James A. Levine in *Psychology Today,* June 1978

kid (coll.) child **vs.** (short for versus) against **average** standard; usual **adult** ['ædʌlt] grown-up **pediatrician** [ˌpiːdɪə'trɪʃən] doctor who specialises in the illnesses of children **psychologist** [saɪ'kɒlədʒɪst] **hence** from now **to ponder** consider; think over **concern** interest or anxiety **grade** a level of the school course **suburban** in an outlying district of a town **to review** consider or examine again **to fit** have the right standard, size, etc. **myth** conventional belief(s) **to depict** describe in words or pictures **composition** structure

8. Bringing up Mother

Sally Norton is known to her friends as a "natural mother". Composed and in command, she appears pleased with her parental role. Even when Ross, her two-year-old, is tired and at his worst, she is able to deal with him calmly and with affection.

On the other hand, Fran Marks, Sally's neighbor and mother of 18-month-old Patsy, seems to be in a state of constant tension and irritation. She is impatient with her daughter, is easily angered by her, and, in the quiet of late evening, appears distracted and depressed.

Both Sally and Fran have always been regarded as stable, competent adults, able to handle stress and change without great cost. Both are secure in their marriages, untroubled by financial pressures, and planning ultimately to return to their careers. Both approached their new parental roles eagerly.

The difference between Sally and Fran as mothers lies not in their own personalities, but in those of their children. Ross is a contented child – easy to care for, sleeping and eliminating on schedule, smiling readily, and offering his parents positive feedback for their efforts in his behalf. In contrast, Patsy is "always cranky", cries easily, is a tiny insomniac, and appears displeased even with heroic attempts to calm and amuse her. In sharply different ways, each mother is being shaped by her child's temperament and behavior.

The two case histories demonstrate a fact of life long overlooked: to a surprising degree, parents are the product of the children born to them. It has been generally accepted, and with good evidence, that parents help mold the child – that a youngster's characteristics are shaped significantly by parental influence. Investigators have rarely considered that the influence might also run the other way – that the child might act upon the mother and the father, might even be responsible for the kind of parental treatment he or she receives.

Julius Segal and Herbert Yahraes in *Psychology Today,* November 1978

composed calm **in command** h. with feelings under control **affection** kindly feeling; love **tension** mental strain or excitement **irritation** anger; annoyance **distracted** confused **stable** balanced **without great cost** not causing too much suffering **secure** free from anxiety **ultimately** finally; in the end **contented** satisfied **to eliminate** h. dirty o.'s nappies **on schedule** regularly **feedback** reaction; response **cranky** (coll.) eccentric; unsteady **insomniac** s.o. who cannot sleep **to mold** give a shape or form to **investigator** s.o. who examines or inquires into s.th. **to act upon** have an effect upon

9. Take5 – deciding which game to use

The teacher must take many factors into account when deciding which game would be most appropriate and most successful with his students at any one time. Primarily he will consider the level of the students but also:

1 What is the main aim of having a game? Is it for specific language or skill practice, for general practice, for relaxation or to punctuate a long lesson?
2 What will interest the students? Are they young or old, serious-minded or light-hearted, highly motivated to learn English or not? Would they prefer an imaginative game or a logical problem-solving game?
3 When is the game to be used? Student motivation and interest in a game may be very different on a Tuesday morning from late on a Friday afternoon, for example. Similarly, students' response to a game after a test or grammar practice session will be different to that after a discussion lesson.

Having considered these factors an initial choice of game should only be confirmed if the teacher is certain it is feasible in the classroom. In other words, the teacher should ensure that the aids and materials are available, students are able to cope with the requirements of the game, such as working in groups, and the linguistic demands the game makes are within the students' capabilities.

Centre for British Teachers

to take into account consider **appropriate** suitable; right for the purpose or occasion **primarily** in the first place **skill** ability to do s.th. expertly and well **relaxation** rest from work or effort **to punctuate** interrupt from time to time **imaginative** [ɪ'mædʒnətɪv]; G. phantasievoll **similarly** likewise, in the same way **response** reaction **initial** first **to confirm** prove to be suitable **feasible** practicable **aid** thing that helps **available** at hand **to cope with** manage successfully **requirement** s.th. that is needed **linguistic** concerning (the scientific study of) language **demand** s. th. which s.o. is asked to do

10. Battle of Trafalgar

Naval engagement of the Napoleonic Wars (1800–15), which established British naval supremacy for more than 100 years; it was fought on Oct. 21, 1805, west of Cape Trafalgar, Spain, between Cádiz and the Strait of Gibraltar. A fleet of 33 ships (18 French and 15 Spanish) under Admiral Pierre de Villeneuve fought a British fleet of 27 ships under Admiral Horatio Nelson.

At the end of September, Villeneuve had received orders to leave Cádiz and land troops at Naples to support the French campaign in southern Italy. On October 19–20 his fleet slipped out of Cádiz, hoping to get into the Mediterranean Sea without giving battle. Nelson caught him off Cape Trafalgar on October 21.

Villeneuve ordered his fleet to form a single line heading north, and Nelson ordered his fleet to form two squadrons and attack Villeneuve's line from the west. By noon the larger squadron, led by Adm. Cuthbert Collingwood in the "Royal Sovereign", had engaged the rear 16 ships of the French-Spanish line. At 11:50 am Nelson in the "Victory", signalled his famous message: "England expects that every man will do his duty." Then his squadron, with 12 ships, attacked the van and centre of Villeneuve's line. The majority of Nelson's squadron broke through and shattered Villeneuve's line in the pell-mell battle. Six of the leading French and Spanish ships were ignored in the first attack and about 3:30 pm were able to turn about to aid those behind. But this weak counterattack failed and was driven off. Collingwood completed the destruction of the rear, and the battle ended about 5:00 pm. Villeneuve himself was captured; and his fleet lost 19 or 20 ships – which were surrendered to the British – and 14,000 men, of whom half were prisoners of war. Nelson was mortally wounded by a sniper, but when he died at 4:30 pm he was certain of his complete victory. About 1,500

British seamen were killed or wounded, but no British ships were lost. Trafalgar shattered forever Napoleon's plans to invade England.

Encyclopaedia Britannica

naval concerning a navy or ships of war **engagement** a battle **supremacy** the highest position of power **cape** a piece of land joined to the coast and standing out into the sea **strait** narrow passage of water connecting two seas **to slip out** leave unnoticed **squadron** a large group of warships **sovereign** a ruler such as a king or queen **rear** the back **van** the leading group of ships in a battle **pell-mell** disorderly **mortally wounded** wounded in a manner resulting in death **sniper** s.o. who shoots from a hidden position; G. Heckenschütze **to shatter** destroy

Chapter III

Point of View

Introductory Remarks

Point of view refers to the way a story is told. The author selects a specific mode of presenting the characters, action, setting and events of his or her narrative. Sometimes the text includes a narrator proper as mediator between story and readers, as someone who guides the readers and influences them in their reception of the text. Sometimes the events are seen through the eyes of one of the characters who thus adopts the function of the narrator.

The degree of insight or penetration the narrators have into the characters and events of a text varies, forming a graded line from *telling* – the narrators know everything and impart their knowledge to the readers as they think fit – to *showing* – the narrators are practically absent and the readers have to infer everything from the events as they unfold. The narrators may either speak in the first or third person without any basic change to their roles. A classification according to their degree of insight would, therefore, appear to be most useful and relevant.

1. Omniscient or unlimited point of view

The narrators know everything that has ever happened or will happen. They have a complete insight into all their characters, their motivations and feelings. They do not themselves participate in the story, but view from outside, supplying their comments and evaluations and even directly addressing the readers from their vantage points. They are not obliged to adhere to the chronology of events, and can employ elements of flashback and anticipation to heighten the tension. They can also move freely among the different locations and events. They normally speak in the first person.

2. Limited point of view

The narrators are the protagonists in the stories. They are restricted in their knowledge to what they can possibly know without violating the rules of probability. The function of narrating a story can also be split up between two or more characters in the text, who give different evaluations of the same events. This can also be achieved by means of letters and messages, for example.

a) Central consciousness

The narrators are the main protagonists of the stories. The events are told as they experience them. The readers acquire an insight into the protagonists' states of mind, but not into those of the other characters. Everything is seen and evaluated according to its impact and effect on the consciousness of these leading characters through whose eyes the readers follow the course of events. In order to establish an increasingly close relationship between reader and protagonist the latter's psyche can be revealed either in the form of reported thought (3rd person narrator, past tense), interior monologue (1st person narrator, complete sentences, logically structured and dealing with a coherent set of themes) or stream of consciousness (1st person narrator, violation of grammatically correct syntax structure; apparently erratic thoughts based on association).

b) Minor character

The narrators are unimportant characters who do not themselves take an active part in the action but who view and evaluate everything from the stance of witnesses on the periphery. Since their task is primarily to report, they are not fully characterized.

3. Eliminated narrator

Characters, action, setting and events are presented directly without the interference of a narrator. The characters reveal themselves through action and speech. They can comment on one another in their speech, but it is left to the reader to decide on the justification or legitimacy of these evaluations.

1. What do we learn about the narrator and what is the narrator's relation to the characters and events?
2. What are the advantages and limitations of the point of view in each text? Please pay particular attention to the relation of the reader to the text.

Useful Phrases

1. The narrator | views… from a distance.
   | stands back from the action and observes.
   | remains outside the plot, merely observing.
2. His lack of involvement permits the narrator to maintain an analytical stance.
3. The narrator describes the action and characters objectively.
4. The story is narrated in the third person, and the narrator never surfaces.
5. There is no interference by the narrator throughout the text.

6.	The narrator	is not involved explicitly.
		is a thinly-sketched character on the edge of the story.

7.	The narrator	plays a more active role in	the text.
		meddles in	
		intervenes in	
		pronounces judgment on	

8.	The narrator	takes part in	…
		is involved in	
		is one of	
		cannot escape from	

9. The narrator is simultaneously a central character in the story.
10. The story is told from the narrator's angle.
11. The fact that the narrator is involved results in the narration being biased and slanted.
12. The narrator's views are committed because of his/her participation in the plot.
13. The narrator describes the event from the point of view of…
14. The narrator's attitude towards his or her material is…
15. The events are viewed from a subjective angle.

16.	The description is	restricted	to…
		limited	

17. The narrator's relation to the text is confined to…
18. The narrator's views are as subjective as those of the others.

19.	The narrator	intends	to	influence	the reader.
		wants		manipulate	
		seeks			

20.	The narrator's introductory remarks also	include	…
		deal with	
		refer to	

21. The points of view in the text shift from character to character.
22. The intention of this narrative approach is…

1. Tom Jones

Reader, I think proper, before we proceed any farther together, to acquaint thee, that I intend to digress, through this whole history, as often as I see occasion: of which I am myself a better judge than any pitiful critic whatever. And here I must desire all those critics to mind their own business, and not to intermeddle with affairs, or works, which no ways concern them: for, till they produce the authority by which they are constituted judges, I shall plead to their jurisdiction.

I have told my reader, in the preceding chapter, that Mr. Allworthy inherited a large fortune; that he had a good heart, and no family. Hence, doubtless, it will be concluded by many, that he lived like an honest man, owed no one a shilling, took nothing but what was his own, kept a good house, entertained his neighbours with a hearty welcome at his table, and was charitable to the poor, i.e. to those who had rather beg than work, by giving them the offals from it; that he dy'd immensely rich, and built an hospital.

And true is, that he did many of these things; but, had he done nothing more, I should have left him to have recorded his own merit on some fair free-stone over the door of that hospital. Matters of a much more extraordinary kind are to be subject of this history, or I should grossly misspend my time in writing so voluminous a work.

Henry Fielding (1749)

to digress (of a writer or speaker) turn aside or wander from the subject **to intermeddle** (obs.) meddle; interfere **to inherit** receive property, title, etc. left by s.o. who has died **hence** therefore; for this reason **charitable** giving freely and generously to the needy **offals** h. leftovers from a meal **free-stone** any kind of building stone that can be easily cut **voluminous** very large

2. Plants in the Home

Basic Rules

Don't drown them. Roots need air as well as water.

Give them a rest. Beginners are usually surprised to learn that nearly all plants need a rest in winter.

Give them extra humidity. The atmosphere of a centrally-heated room in winter is as dry as desert air.

Treat trouble promptly. Learn to recognise the early signs of trouble.

Group them together. Nearly all plants look better and grow better when grouped together.

Learn to repot.

Choose wisely. The plant must be able to flourish in the home you provide for it.

Dr. D. J. Hessayon, *The House Plant Expert* (1980)

humidity the amount of water in the air **to repot** [ˌriːˈpɒt] **to flourish** [ʌ] h. grow healthily

3. The Prologue to *Romeo and Juliet*

Enter Chorus

Chorus. Two households both alike in dignity
(In fair Verona, where we lay our scene)
From ancient grudge break to new mutiny,
Where civil blood makes civil hands unclean.
From forth the fatal loins of these two foes
A pair of star-cross'd lovers take their life,
Whose misadventur'd piteous overthrows
Doth with their death bury their parents' strife.
The fearful passage of their death-mark'd love
And the continuance of their parents' rage,
Which, but their children's end, nought could remove,
Is now the two hours' traffic of our stage;
The which, if you with patient ears attend,
What here shall miss, our toil shall strive to mend.

Exit.

William Shakespeare, *Romeo and Juliet*, I, 1, 1–14 (1594/5)

grudge a cause for dislike, feeling of anger **mutiny** h. quarrel **loins** G. Lenden **star-cross'd** ill-fated **misadventur'd** caused by bad luck **piteous** ['pɪtɪəs] causing pity **doth** (obs.) does **strife** trouble between people **but** h. except for **nought** (obs.) [nɔːt] nothing **traffic** h. action **toil** hard work

4. Sense and Sensibility

Mr. John Dashwood had not the strong feelings of the rest of the family; but he was affected by a recommendation of such a nature at such a time, and he promised to do every thing in his power to make them comfortable. His father was rendered easy by such an assurance, and Mr. John Dashwood had then leisure to consider how much there might prudently be in his power to do for them.

He was not an ill-disposed young man, unless to be rather cold hearted, and rather selfish, is to be ill-disposed: but he was, in general, well respected; for he conducted himself with propriety in the discharge of his ordinary duties. Had he married a more amiable woman, he might have been made still more respectable than he was: – he might even have been made amiable himself; for he was very young when he married, and very fond of his wife. But Mrs. John Dashwood was a strong caricature of himself; – more narrow-minded and selfish.

When he gave his promise to his father, he meditated within himself to increase the fortunes of his sisters by the present of a thousand pounds a-piece. He then really thought himself equal to it. The prospect of four thousand a-year, in addition to his present income, besides the remaining half of his own mother's fortune, warmed his heart and made him feel capable of generosity. – "Yes, he would give them three thousand pounds: it would be liberal and handsome! It would be enough to make them completely easy. Three thousand pounds! he could spare so considerable a sum with little inconvenience." – He thought of it all day long, and for many days successively, and he did not repent.

Jane Austen (1811)

recommendation h. attractive quality **to be rendered easy** make one feel unworried **assurance** promise **prudent** sensible and wise **ill-disposed** with an unpleasant character or bad qualities **propriety** [prə'praɪətɪ] correctness of social or moral behaviour **discharge** performance **amiable** ['eɪmjəbl] of a pleasant nature; friendly **caricature** ['kærɪkətjʊə] **a-piece** each **to be equal to s.th.** be able to deal or cope with s.th. **generosity** readiness to give money, help, etc. **liberal** large; given freely **inconvenience** difficulty **successive** one after the other **to repent** h. be dissatisfied or regretful about

5. The Loneliness of the Long-Distance Runner

As soon as I got to Borstal they made me a long-distance cross-country runner. I suppose they thought I was just the build for it because I was long and skinny for my age (and still am) and in any case I didn't mind it much, to tell you the truth, because running had always been made much of in our family, especially running away from the police. I've always been a good runner, quick and with a big stride as well, the only trouble being that no matter how fast I run, and I did a very fair lick even though I do say so myself, it didn't stop me getting caught by the cops after that bakery job.

You might think it a bit rare, having long-distance cross-country runners in Borstal, thinking that the first thing a long-distance cross-country runner would do when they set him loose at them fields and woods would be to run as far away from the place as he could get on a bellyful of Borstal slumgullion – but you're wrong, and I'll tell you why.

The first thing is that them bastards over us aren't as daft as they most of the time look, and for another thing I'm not so daft as I would look if I tried to make a break for it on my long-distance running, because to abscond and then get caught is nothing but a mug's game, and I'm not falling for it. Cunning is what counts in this life, and even that you've got to use in the slyest way you can; I'm telling you straight: they're cunning, and I'm cunning.

Alan Sillitoe (1958)

borstal prison for young people **cross-country** (race run) across fields or open country **build** shape and size **skinny** (sl.) thin **to make much of** treat as important **stride** a long step **to do a fair lick** (sl.) run very fast **cop** (sl.) policeman **job** (sl.) h. G. Ding **them** (coll.) **fields** those fields **on a bellyful of Borstal slumgullion** ['slʌm'gʌlɪən] G. mit einem Bauchvoll Borstal Schlangenfraß **daft** (sl.) silly; foolish **to abscond** (fml.) h. escape from prison **a mug's game** (sl.) an action that is unlikely to be profitable **to fall for** accept and be cheated by **cunning** showing or having cleverness in deceiving **sly** clever in deceiving

6. A Visit of Charity

There was loose, bulging linoleum on the floor. Marian felt as if she were walking on the waves, but the nurse paid no attention to it. There was a smell in the hall like the interior of a clock. Everything was silent until, behind one of the doors, an old lady of some kind cleared her throat like a sheep bleating. This decided the nurse. Stopping in her tracks, she first extended her arm, bent her elbow, and leaned forward from the hips – all to examine the watch strapped to her wrist; then she gave a loud double tap on the door.

"There are two in each room," the nurse remarked over her shoulder.

"Two what?" asked Marian without thinking. The sound like a sheep's bleating almost made her turn around and run back.

One old woman was pulling the door open in short, gradual jerks, and when she saw the nurse a strange smile forced her old face dangerously awry. Marian, suddenly propelled by the strong, impatient arm of the nurse, saw next the side-face of another old woman, even older, who was lying flat in bed with a cap on and a counterpane drawn up to her chin.

"Visitor," said the nurse, and after one more shove she was off up the hall.

Marian stood tongue-tied; both hands held the potted plant. The old woman, still with that terrible, square smile (which was a smile of welcome) stamped on her bony face, was waiting… Perhaps she said something. The old woman in bed said nothing at all, and she did not look around.

Suddenly Marian saw a hand, quick as a bird claw, reach up in the air and pluck the white cap off her head. At the same time, another claw to match drew her all the way into the room, and the next moment the door closed behind her.

"My, my, my," said the old lady at her side.

Marian stood enclosed by a bed a washstand and a chair; the tiny room had altogether too much furniture. Everything smelled wet – even the bare floor. She held onto the back of the chair, which was wicker and felt soft and damp. Her heart beat more and more slowly, her hands got colder and colder, and she could not hear whether the old women were saying anything or not. She could not see them very clearly. How dark it was! The window shade was down, and the only door was shut. Marian looked at the ceiling. It was like being caught in a robbers' cave just before one was murdered.

Eudora Welty (1941)

bulging swelling **to bleat** make a sound like a sheep, goat, etc. **in o.'s tracks** where one is; abruptly **jerk** short sharp strong pull **awry** [ə'raɪ] twisted; out of shape **to propel** [prə'pel] move, dive or push forward **counterpane** ornamental blanket spread over a bed **shove** [ʃʌv] strong push **claw** G. Klaue **to pluck** pull sharply **to match** (short for 'to match the other') similar **wicker** G. Korb- **damp** rather wet

7. A Portrait of the Artist as a Young Man

How far away they were! There was cold sunlight outside the window. He wondered if he would die. You could die just the same on a sunny day. He might die before his mother came. Then he would have a dead mass in the chapel like the way the fellows had told him it was when Little had died. All the fellows would be at the mass, dressed in black, all with sad faces. Wells too would be there but no fellow would look at him. The rector would be there in a cope of black and gold and there would be tall yellow candles on the altar and round the catafalque. And they would carry the coffin out of the chapel slowly and he would be buried in the little graveyard of the community off the main avenue of limes. And Wells would be sorry then for what he had done. And the bell would toll slowly.

James Joyce (1916)

dead mass G. Totenmesse **cope** a long loose gown worn by priests on special occasions **catafalque** raised framework for the coffin before a funeral **lime** G. Linde **to toll** [təʊl] ring slowly and repeatedly

8. A Tradition of Eighteen Hundred and Four

The widely discussed possibility of an invasion of England through a Channel tunnel has more than once recalled old Solomon Selby's story to my mind.

The occasion on which I numbered myself among his audience was one evening when he was sitting in the yawning chimney-corner of the inn-kitchen, with some others who had gathered there, and I entered for shelter from the rain. Withdrawing the stem of his pipe from the dental notch in which it habitually rested, he leaned back in the recess behind him and smiled into the fire. The smile was neither mirthful nor sad, not precisely humorous nor altogether thoughtful. We who knew him recognized it in a moment: it was his narrative smile. Breaking off our few desultory remarks we drew up closer, and he thus began: –

'My father, as you mid know, was a shepherd all his life, and lived out by the Cove four miles yonder, where I was born and lived likewise, till I moved here shortly afore I was married.

Thomas Hardy (1888)

yawning h. wide **dental notch** gap between teeth **habitual** usual; customary **recess** ['riːses] space in the wall (usu. for shelves, etc.) **mirthful** merry **narrative** ['nærətɪv] **smile** smile indicating intention to tell a story **desultory** casual; G. beiläufig **mid** (dial.) might **yonder** over there **afore** before

9. Royal praise

The Queen congratulated 4,000 members of the Boys' Brigade from throughout Britain yesterday in a royal review at Edinburgh marking 100 years of the brigade.

Martina's day

Martina Navratilova took only 54 minutes to win her fourth Wimbledon singles title, worth £60,000, by beating Andrea Jaeger 6–0, 6–3.

The Observer, 3 July 1983

10. Hills like White Elephants

The hills across the valley of the Ebro were long and white. On this side there was no shade and no trees and the station was between two lines of rails in the sun. Close against the side of the station there was the warm shadow of the building and a curtain, made of strings of bamboo beads, hung across the open door into the bar, to keep out flies. The American and the girl with him sat at a table in the shade, outside the building. It was very hot and the express from Barcelona would come in forty minutes. It stopped at this junction for two minutes and went on to Madrid.

'What should we drink?' the girl asked. She had taken off her hat and put it on the table.

'It's pretty hot,' the man said.

'Let's drink beer.'

'Dos cervezas,' the man said into the curtain.

'Big ones?' a woman asked from the doorway.

'Yes. Two big ones.'

The woman brought two glasses of beer and two felt pads. She put the felt pads and the beer glasses on the table and looked at the man and the girl. The girl was looking off at the line of hills. They were white in the sun and the country was brown and dry.

'They look like white elephants,' she said.

'I've never seen one,' the man drank his beer.

'No, you wouldn't have.'

'I might have,' the man said. 'Just because you say I wouldn't have doesn't prove anything.'

The girl looked at the bead curtain. 'They've painted something on it,' she said. 'What does it say?'

'Anis del Toro. It's a drink.'

'Could we try it?'

The man called 'Listen' through the curtain. The woman came out from the bar.

Ernest Hemingway (1927)

Ebro longest river in Spain **felt pad** G. Filzuntersetzer

11. New Year's deadly night of panic

Two die, 500 hurt as crowd push and fight

The traditional New Year's Eve celebration in Trafalgar Square plunged into grim tragedy soon after midnight yesterday when two women were trampled to death and hundreds of people injured in the surging, panic-stricken crowd.

The disorder and confusion that occurred have led to demands for an investigation into the arrangements made by police and other bodies for handling the annual gathering in the square. Over 500 people were treated at St. John Ambulance mobile first-aid centres at the square, and 141 people were taken to hospital. …

"All of a sudden it seemed everyone was panicking," a London Ambulance Service spokesman said. "People at the back pushed forward, and the more they pushed, the more the people at the front pushed back. Then the barrier gave way and the two women fell. The crowd just trampled them to death."

By late evening yesterday only one of the dead had been publicly identified. Police had the name of the other woman and were trying to trace the next of kin. She is a 24-year-old girl from South Africa.

There was still a good deal of uncertainty late yesterday over exactly what happened when the huge crowd started to stream out of the square a few minutes after the chimes of Big Ben had heralded the arrival of 1983.

The ambulance spokesman said the stampede started when people tried to move out of the way to allow an ambulance crew with a doctor to reach a policeman who had fallen into a basement well. Others in the square told of drunken gangs of youths conga-dancing into the tightly-packed crowd.

It was clear, however, that there had been little liaison between the Department of the Environment, which controls the square, Scotland Yard, responsible for maintaining public order, and Westminster Council, which is in charge of the area around the square.

Sunday Times, 2 January 1983 (abridged)

to plunge h. turn suddenly into **to surge** move, esp. forward, in or like powerful waves **body** h. authority **mobile** ['məʊbaɪl] **next of kin** closest relative(s) **chime** sound made by a set of bells **to herald** announce **stampede** a sudden mad rush **basement well** an enclosed space containing a staircase leading to a flat below street level **conga** G. Polonaise **liaison** [liː'eɪzɒn] co-operation **Department of the Environment** authority responsible for housing, environmental protection, town planning **to be in charge of s.th.** be responsible for s.th.

12. Macbeth

SCENE V. – *Inverness.* MACBETH'S *Castle.*
Enter LADY MACBETH, *reading a letter.*

They met me in the day of success; and I have learned by the perfectest report, they have more in them than mortal knowledge. When I burned in desire to question them further, they made themselves air, into which they vanished. Whiles I stood rapt in the wonder of it, came missives from the king, who all-hailed me, 'Thane of Cawdor'; by which title, before, these weird sisters saluted me, and referred me to the coming on of time, with, 'Hail, king that shalt be!' This have I thought good to deliver thee, my dearest partner of greatness, that thou mightest not lose the dues of rejoicing, by being ignorant of what greatness is promised thee. Lay it to thy heart, and farewell.

Glamis thou art, and Cawdor; and shalt be
What thou art promis'd. Yet do I fear thy nature;
It is too full o' the milk of human kindness
To catch the nearest way; thou wouldst be great,
Art not without ambition, but without
The illness should attend it; what thou wouldst highly,
That thou wouldst holily; wouldst not play false,
And yet wouldst wrongly win; thou'dst have, great Glamis,
That which cries, 'Thus thou must do, if thou have it';
And that which rather thou dost fear to do
Than wishest should be undone. Hie thee hither,
That I may pour my spirits in thine ear,
And chastise with the valour of my tongue
All that impedes thee from the golden round,
Which fate and metaphysical aid doth seem
To have thee crown'd withal.

William Shakespeare, *Macbeth* I, 5, 1–31 (1605/6)

perfectest (obs.) most perfect **rapt** very absorbed **missive** ['mɪsɪv] h. messenger **to hail** greet with respect **thane** a low-ranking noble in Scottish history **weird sister** witch **shalt** (obs.) shall **thou mightest** (obs.) you may; thou/thee, G. du/dir, dich **due** s.th. rightfully belonging to s.o. **Glamis** [glɑːmz] thane of Glamis **art** (obs.) are **o'** of **to attend** h. go with **hie thee hither** come here quickly **chastise** [tʃæs'taɪz] blame severely **valour** bravery **to impede** hinder **golden round** (golden) crown **metaphysical** supernatural **withal** with

13. The Lapse

At 4.13 Henry showed his season ticket to the porter and climbed into the railway car. He nodded politely to Miss Burge, the teacher at the kindergarten, who sat in her corner seat knitting the green jumper she had started last month; and to the district nurse in her black pork-pie hat, her professional bag tucked warmly against her stomach. They both smiled back – nothing said, never anything said – and he went to his usual place at the far end of the car. He filled his pipe while waiting for the train to start, and then put it back into his pocket.

Back and fore, back and fore, like a shuttle, workwards each morning, homewards each night, ra-ta-ta, ra-ta-ta, the train's travelling beat – how many times have I done this journey, these last five years? If I put the journeys end to end it would stretch a long way – right into Tibet perhaps, along the Turk-Sib, among the moujiks... Oh dear! Henry yawned and gazed indifferently at the row of slatternly back gardens and flapping clothes lines past which the train ran. Twice a day for five years, Bank holidays excepted, those drab hotchpotch backs where the wives riddled yesterday's ashes and the children sat on the steps eating bread and jam. It was so depressing to see those streets every day, always the same, and the people always the same – how many of them knew they had been condemned to serve a lifer?

And then, with a rattle and a wrench, the open country; the hills swooping like swallows. Below the embankment the black river swirled, wandering down from the coal mines at the head of the valley. And the train rattled over the bridge that spanned the river; Henry felt the drop under the bridge, sheer and empty in the pit of his stomach, like a bird flashing through a hollow cave. And on, accelerando, through the cutting. What shall I do tonight, the tired voice asked in his head. Pictures? Or a nap and a stroll down to the billiard hall? I don't know what to do, I can never make up my mind.

Alun Lewis (1942)

pork-pie hat hat with a flat round top and a brim **to tuck** hold tightly **shuttle** G. Schiffchen am Webrahmen **Turk-Sib** Turkish-Siberian Railway **moujik** ['mu:ʒ'ik] Russian peasant **slatternly** (adj.) untidy **bank holiday** official public holiday on weekdays **drab hotchpotch back** shabby disorderly back garden **to riddle ashes** shake the grate (G. Rost) to separate the ashes from the coal **to serve a lifer** be a lifetime in prison **wrench** h. violent movement **to swoop** ascend and descend sharply **embankment** wall of earth or stone built to keep a river from overflowing; can also carry a railway line **to swirl** flow with twisting movements **drop** h. depth **accelerando** at increased speed **cutting** passage dug in the ground for a railway to pass **nap** short sleep **stroll** leisurely walk

14. Ulysses

Yes because he never did a thing like that before a ask to get his breakfast in bed with a couple of eggs since the City Arms hotel when he used to be pretending to be laid up with a sick voice doing his highness to make himself interesting for that old faggot Mrs. Riordan that he thought he had a great leg of and she never left us a farthing all for masses for herself and her soul greatest miser ever was actually afraid to lay out 4d for her methylated spirit telling me all her ailments she had too much old chat in her about politics and earthquakes and the end of the world let us have a bit of fun first God help the world if all the women were her sort down on bathingsuits and lownecks of course nobody wanted her to wear them I suppose she was pious because no man would look at her twice I hope Ill never be like her a wonder she didnt want us to cover our faces but she was a welleducated woman certainly and her gabby talk about Mr. Riordan here and Mr. Riordan there I suppose he was glad to get shut of her and her dog smelling my fur and always edging to get up under my petticoats especially then still I like that in him polite to old women like that and waiters and beggars too hes not proud out of nothing but not always if ever he got anything really serious the matter with him its much better for them to go into a hospital where everything is clean but I suppose Id have to dring it into him for a month yes and then wed have a hospital nurse next thing on the carpet have him staying there till they throw him out or a nun maybe like the smutty photo he has shes as much a nun as Im not yes because theyre so weak and puling when theyre sick they want a woman to get well if his nose bleeds youd think it was O tragic and that dyinglooking one off the south circular when he sprained his foot at the choir party at the sugarloaf Mountain the day I wore that dress Miss Stack bringing him flowers the worst old ones she could find at the bottom of the basket anything at all to get into a mans bedroom with her old maids voice trying to imagine he was dying on account of her

James Joyce (1922)

to be laid up (coll.) forced to stay in bed (due to illness) **to do one's highness** pretend to be an eminent person **faggot** (sl.) pej. old ugly woman **to have a great leg of** be favoured by s.o. **farthing** former British coin worth a quarter of an old penny **miser** extremely mean and greedy person **4d** four old pennies **methylated spirit** G. Brennspiritus **ailment** aches and pains **lownecks** women wearing clothes with a low neckline **pious** strictly religious **gabby** (coll.) gossipy **to get shut of s.o.** get rid of s.o. **to edge** come slowly nearer **to dring** force into **wed** we'd **smutty** obscene **to pule** cry **to sprain** injure by sudden twisting **sugarloaf Mountain** large hill near Dublin

Chapter IV

Plot and Characters

Introductory Remarks

The plot of a text is not to be equated with the summary of a text. The plot is the logical, causal construction of setting (time, place, environment), action (in the character's mind or externally), and characters in a text; the summary is only a chronological presentation. Thus, plot is concerned with the interrelationship of characters, setting, and events, not merely with their position in the text. It is an "ordered structure of action" (Abrams), and the success of a plot depends on how effectively the component parts are linked. In a plot neither characters, events, nor setting are redundant but rather contribute to the unity of a text's structure. Obviously, the intention behind a text determines the selection and significance of components and the kind of order given to them.

The main character in a text is called the protagonist. Should he or she be contrasted with another main character, in this case the antagonist, there emerges a conflict. The presentation of this conflict is achieved through the interplay of characters and events. However, the focus of attention is ultimately not really pointed towards an individual character, but towards more fundamental human experience, such as love/hate, life/death, meaning/absurdity of life; and broader cultural questions of society, religion, ethics.

Characters are the persons presented in a text, and they are interpreted by the reader as having inner qualities and attitudes that are expressed either in what they say and do (i.e. by means of dialogue and action) or in the information given to the reader by the narrator.

These two modes of presentation are called showing and telling. In showing, the characters are merely presented talking and acting, and the reader is asked to interpret what motives and dispositions lie behind what they say and do. In this context the following methods of characterization are relevant:

- A character presents himself or herself in a monologue.
- Characters indirectly reveal personal features in a dialogue on a topic or problem.

- Characters are characterized by the way they speak and/or by what they do.
- A character is directly described by others.

In telling, the narrator intervenes authoritatively in order to describe, and often to evaluate, the motives and dispositional qualities of the characters.

The mode of presenting a character largely depends on the point of view. Normally, showing is associated with the eliminated narrator, telling with the omniscient or unlimited narrator. (See theoretical section on point of view for further details.) However, these modes of presentation are often to be found combined in one text.

Another distinction should be made between flat and round characters. A flat character (also called type or two-dimensional) is "constructed round a single idea or quality" (E. M. Forster) and is presented without much individualizing detail, and therefore can be fairly adequately described in a single phrase or sentence. Individual features are presented in a rough sketch only. Normally, a flat character does not undergo any development, remaining essentially stable.

A round character is complex in temperament and motivation and is presented with subtle particularity. Round characters are capable of development and of changing their moral and ethical attitudes (dynamic characters).

The degree to which characters need to be presented in detail depends on their function in the plot.

I (Texts 1–8)

1. Who is characterized in each of the texts or text extracts? Give a short characterization in your own words.
2. What method of characterization is employed in each case? Discuss the effectiveness of each of the methods of characterization.
3. Creative writing: characterize a person of your own choice using the two methods of presentation, telling and showing.

II (Text 9)

1. Give a plot outline of the story.
2. Discuss the different types of character in the short story and how they are characterized.
3. Describe the story's setting and its relevance to both plot and characters.

Useful Phrases

1. to	reveal uncover disclose	individual features of a character

2. to depict the	main prominent	features of a person

3. The narrator describes the dominant	characteristics features traits	of a character.

4. During the course of the	novel play poem	the character undergoes a development.

5. The character remains essentially unchanged.

6. The character changes his/her attitude.

7. to	use employ	telling showing	as a mode of characterization

8. The narrator presents his/her characters.

9. The narrator	gives presents	a rough	sketch description	of s.o.'s character.

10. to give a	faithful realistic detailed	description characterization	of s.o.

11. to convey a	vivid impressive	portrayal of…

12. to	describe picture	a character realistically

13. to	portray characterize	s.o. with attention to detail

14. The description	presents includes contains	many details.

15. to	give supply convey	an impression

16. to point out the characteristics of s.o.

17. to characterize a person as…

18. to	present provide	a portrait of a person

19. to caricature a person

20. to present a stereotyped person

21. to give a detailed analysis of s.o.

22. The narrator is particularly interested in the psychology of a character.

23. In this description the narrator intends to convey the impression that...

24. The narrator gives / provides / presents some typical details.

25. An essential component of this character is...

1. Chips with Everything

ACT ONE

Scene one

An R. A. F. hut.

[*Nine new conscripts enter. They are subdued, uncertain, mumbling.* Corporal Hill *appears at door, stocky, Northern, collarless man. He waits till they notice him, which they gradually do till mumbling ceases, utterly – they rise to attention. After a long pause*]

Hill: That's better. In future, whenever an N.C.O. comes into the hut, no matter who he is, the first person to see him will call out 'N.C.O.! N.C.O.!' like that. And whatever you're doing, even if you're stark bollock naked, you'll all spring to attention as fast as the wind from a duck's arse, and by Christ that's fast. Is that understood? [*No reply.*] Well is it? [*A few murmurs.*] When I ask a question I expect an answer. [*Emphatically*] Is that understood!

All [*shouting*]: Yes, Corporal!

Hill: Anyone been in the Air Cadets? Any of the cadets? Anyone twenty-one or more then? Nineteen? [*Two boys,* Andrew *and* Dickey, *raise their hands. To one*] Month you were born?

Andrew: July, Corporal.

Dickey: May, Corporal.

Hill: [*to* Dickey]: You're senior man. [*To* Andrew] You're assistant. Shift your kit to top of hut. Not now – later.

[Hill *scrutinizes the rest. He lays his hand on the two smallest –* Dodger *and* Ginger.]

These small boys, these two, they're my boys. They'll do the jobs I ask them when I ask them; not much, my fires each day, perhaps my bunk

– my boys. But they won't do my polishing – I do that myself. No one is to start on them, no one is to bully them, if they do, then they answer to me. [*Pause.*] You can sit now.

[*Reads out list of names, each recruit rises and sits as called. Boys sit on their beds, waiting;* HILL *paces up and down, waiting his time. Then*] Right, you're in the R.A.F. now, you're not at home. This hut, this place here, this is going to be your home for the next eight scorching weeks. This billet here, you see it? This? It's in a state now, no one's been in it for the last four days so it's in a state now. [*Pause.*] But usually it's like a scorching palace! [*Pause.*] That's the way I want it to be cos that's the way it's always been. Now you've got to get to know me. My name is Corporal Hill. I'm not a very happy man, I don't know why. I never smile and I never joke – you'll soon see that. Perhaps it's my nature, perhaps it's the way I've been brought up – I don't know. The R.A.F. brought me up. You're going to go through hell while you're here, through scorching hell. Some of you will take it and some of you will break down. I'm warning you – some of you shall end up crying. And when that happens I don't want to see anyone laughing at him. Leave him alone, don't touch him.

But I'll play fair. You do me proud and I'll play fair. The last lot we 'ad 'ere 'ad a good time, a right time, a right good scorching time. We 'ad bags o' fun, bags o' it. But I will tear and mercilessly scratch the scorching daylights out of anyone who smarts the alec with me – and we've got some 'ere. I can see them, you can tell them. I count three already, you can tell them, by their faces, who know it all, the boys who think they're GOOD. [*Whispered*] It'll be unmerciful and scorching murder for them – all. Now, you see this wireless here, this thing with knobs and a pretty light that goes on and off? Well that's ours, our wireless for this hut, and for this hut only because this hut has always been the best hut. No other hut has a wireless. I want to keep that. I like music and I want to keep that wireless. Some people, when they get up in the morning, first thing all they want to do is smoke, or drink tea – not me, I've got to have music, the noise of instruments.

Everyone's got a fad, that's mine, music, and I want to be spoilt, you see to it that I'm spoilt. Right, if there's anyone here who wants to leave my hut and go into another because he doesn't like this 'un, then do it now, please. Go on, pick up your kit and move. I'll let 'im. [*No movement.*] You can go to the Naafi now. But be back by ten thirty, cos that's bleedin' lights out. [*Moves to door, pauses.*] Anyone object to swearing? [*No reply. Exit.*]

[*Stunned. A boy rushes in from another hut.*]

BOY: What's your'n say?
SMILER [*imitating*]: My name is Corporal Hill, I'm not a happy man.
BOY [*imitating a Scotsman*]: My name is Corporal Bridle – and I'm a bastard!

Arnold Wesker (1962)

conscript person made to serve in one of the armed forces by law **Corporal** G. Stabsunteroffizier **to subdue** make quieter, gentler **to mumble** speak unclearly **stocky** thick, short, and strong in body **Northern** from the North of England **N.C.O.** (abbr.) non-commissioned officer; G. Unteroffizier **stark bollock** (sl.) completely **kit** clothes, other articles needed by a soldier, sailor, or airman **to scrutinize** examine closely **bunk** simple kind of bed, often found in army camps **to bully** use **bully** use one's strength to hurt weaker people or make them afraid **recruit** s. o. who has just joined the armed forces **scorching** (h. term used for stress and emphasis) absolutely terrible **billet** room where soldiers live and sleep **in a state** untidy; in a mess **cos** because **'ad** had **'ere** here **bags** (coll.) h. lots **to scratch the daylights out of s. o.** (sl.) make life extremely difficult for s.o. **to smart the alec** (coll.) claim to know everything and try to sound clever **knob** round control button **fad** a keenly followed interest, often short-lived **'un** one **Naafi** (abbr.) Navy, army, air force institutes; shop for members of the armed forces **bastard** (derog. sl.) a person one intensely dislikes; (normally, child of unmarried parents)

2. Personal Column

Requests for Friendship

FEMINIST, WEST LONDON, mother, teacher, 36, into CND, Labour Party, would find life more complete with non-smoking, reliable man, to whom looks are immaterial. Box 8974.

GRADUATE WOMAN school teacher, 45, divorced, warm, honest and loving, seeks similar man for close relationship. Interests: music, travel, home-life. London home. Box 8810.

JOYFUL, PRETTY WIDOW,
NW London, art teacher, 5' 8'', seeks a good man (44-56 approx.), practical, friendly and with a sense of humour.
Box 8977

MALE LECTURER, 46, divorced, sensitive, caring, non Tory, interested in the arts and social sciences, seeks attractive, intelligent female, 30s-40s, for sincere relationship. Midlands. Box 8945.

MALE 38, quiet, but likes theatre, music, cinema, would like to meet lady, 27-38, initially for friendship, but hopefully more. London NW2. Box 8972.

MALE 33, usual intellectual pretentions and pastimes, meat eating vegetarian, vast and varied background, wants to meet equally silly, outspoken, honest female. West Yorks. Box 8981.

New Statesman, 10 August 1984

(to be) into s.th. (coll.) interested in **CND** Campaign for Nuclear Disarmament **reliable** trustworthy **immaterial** of no real importance **box** G. Postfach **graduate** possessing a university degree **to be divorced** [dɪ'vɔːst] G. geschieden sein **NW** North West **5'8''** 5 feet and 8 inches, about 1.65 metres **lecturer** s.o. who teaches at a college or university (not a professor) **Tory** a supporter of the Conservative Party **sincere** honest **Midlands** industrial area around the cities of Birmingham, Leeds, Manchester, and Liverpool **pretention** false claim and exaggerated behaviour; G. Dünkel **pastime** hobby **vast** very large **outspoken** showing clearly one's thoughts and feelings **Yorks.** Yorkshire

3. The Mysterious Affair at Styles

In a few moments he had unbarred the door, and I followed him up to his room. There he installed me in a chair, and I related the whole story, keeping back nothing, and omitting no circumstance, however insignificant, whilst he himself made a careful and deliberate toilet.

I told him of my awakening, of Mrs. Inglethorp's dying words, of her husband's absence, of the quarrel the day before, of the scrap of conversation between Mary and her mother-in-law that I had overheard, of the former quarrel between Mrs. Inglethorp and Evelyn Howard, and of the latter's innuendoes.

I was hardly as clear as I could wish. I repeated myself several times, and occasionally had to go back to some detail that I had forgotten. Poirot smiled kindly on me.

"The mind is confused? Is it not so? Take time, *mon ami.* You are agitated; you are excited – it is but natural. Presently, when we are calmer, we will arrange the facts, neatly, each in his proper place. We will examine – and reject. Those of importance we will put on one side; those of no importance, pouf!" – he screwed up his cherub-like face, and puffed comically enough – "blow them away!"

"That's all very well," I objected, "but how are you going to decide what is important, and what isn't? That always seems the difficulty to me."

Poirot shook his head energetically. He was now arranging his moustache with exquisite care.

"Not so. *Voyons!* One fact leads to another – so we continue. Does the next fit in with that? *A merveille!* Good! We can proceed. This next little fact – no! Ah, that is curious! There is something missing – a link in the chain that is not there. We examine. We search. And that little curious fact, that possibly paltry little detail that will not tally, we put it here!" He made an extravagant gesture with his hand. "It is significant! It is tremendous!"

"Y —es——"

"Ah!" Poirot shook his forefinger so fiercely at me that I quailed before it. "Beware! Peril to the detective who says: 'It is so small – it does not matter. It will not agree. I will forget it.' That way lies confusion! Everything matters."

"I know. You always told me that. That's why I have gone into all the details of this thing whether they seemed to me relevant or not."

Agatha Christie (1920)

to unbar open a door; G. entriegeln **to install** place **to omit** leave out **deliberate** slow and cautious **toilet** process of dressing, arranging o.'s hair, etc. **scrap** small piece **to overhear** hear by chance, without the knowledge of the speaker(s) **innuendo** indirect reference, usu. s.th. unfavourable to a person's reputation **agitated** ['ædʒɪteɪtɪd] full of anxiety **to screw up o.'s face** make a funny face, e.g. when going out into bright sunshine from a dark room **cherub** angel, normally presented with a round face **to puff** breathe out quickly and noisily **moustache** [mə'stɑːʃ] hair growing on the upper lip **exquisite** [-'--] h. utmost **Voyons!** French for Let us see! **to fit in with** be suitably related to; conform, belong to **A merveille!** French for Wonderful! **paltry** ['pɔːltrɪ] worthless; of no importance **to tally** [''tælɪ] correspond; fit in with **to quail** feel or show fear **peril** danger

4. Class Enemy

MASTER. *I* remember you.

IRON. Do you cunt?

MASTER. Herron. That's your name. Yes.

Pause.

Do you know Herron that I find people like you the most depressing of the lot. Because you're really very bright aren't you. But you throw it all away. You don't *want* to *know* do you? You just don't want to know.

IRON. Know what cunt?

MASTER. Dumb insolence or downright insolence I tell you I give up.

SNATCH. Please sir I'm sorry sir.

MASTER. Uh?

SNATCH. Please sir I'm sorry sir.

MASTER. What?

SNATCH. 'Bout wot I done on ver wall sir.

MASTER. *What* exactly did you do on the wall Cameron?

SNATCH. My name sir. Snatch sir. I done my name.

MASTER. Well Cameron, I don't know whether this means anything to you but I don't care about the wall. I didn't come here to complain about the wall or about whatever you may have done to it. I didn't actually intend to come here at all Cameron. I *happened* to be passing. Because if you want to know wild horses wouldn't drag me anywhere near this particular hell hole in the normal course of events. And Cameron, after what you little savages have done to the doors, windows and walls of this school I don't think one more name or one more foul word is going to make any difference whatsoever. You see,

Cameron – we've given up caring about what the place looks like. We've given up caring Cameron.
Pause.
I think if we put you lot in the Garden of Eden – in ten minutes you'd have it looking like a slum. If we put you in the middle of Buckingham Palace you'd lay it waste just as speedily and thoroughly as you do this poor benighted, last post of education.

IRON. Yeh. We could cunt. An' yoo know why?

MASTER. No Herron. You tell me why.

IRON. 'Cos ve on'y 'fing we don' lay waste to is ours. An' nuffink's ours. You ain't given us nuffink an' wot you give us you take away at yore convenience. An' as long as you treat us that way we'll lay waste cunt. Books, teachers, winders, doors, walls, floors, we'll lay it all ter waste. 'Till we get sunning thass ours. O.K. cunt?

MASTER. You're not fit for ownership Herron. You're not fit to be trusted with each other. Are you coming Skellett?

SKY-LIGHT. No I ain't.

MASTER. Come on.

SKY-LIGHT. Don' touch me sir. Or like 'e said. You'll get done.

MASTER. Honour among thieves eh? Eh?

SKY-LIGHT. On'y fuckin' place there is any honour. Sir.

MASTER. There. Well I wouldn't expect anyone else. I don't think we've got anyone to send down to you. I think, frankly, that you'd be better off in the streets don't you? Isn't that what the police are for? Because this, in case you hadn't noticed, is a place of learning, a place you come to to acquire knowledge. And it is only the knowledge that you brought in with you that you will take away. The knowledge of how to bully, swear and break. Yes?
Pause.
I give up on you. We give up on you. It's pathetic. Did you know that?

Nigel Williams (1978)

cunt (h. taboo expression of extreme dislike) a nasty person **lot** (coll.) group **dumb** [dʌm] stupid **insolence** disrespect and rudeness **downright** (coll.) h. total, complete **'Bout wot I done on ver wall sir** (sociolect: a kind of language spoken by a particular social group) About what I did on the wall, sir **I done** (socio.) I did (meaning: I wrote) **to drag** pull along with force **savage** normally, a member of an uncivilized tribe or group **to lay s.th. waste** destroy a place **thoroughly** [ˈθʌrəlɪ] (adv.) completely **benighted** surrounded by intellectual and moral darkness **last post** a distant, small, and lonely trading camp far away from civilization **'Cos ve on'y 'fing we don' lay waste to is ours** (socio.) Because the only thing we don't lay waste to is ours **nuffink** (socio.) nothing **You ain't given** (socio.) you haven't given **yore** (socio.) your **winder** (socio.) window **ter** (socio.) to **sunning thass** (socio.) something that's **No I ain't** (socio.) No, I am not **to get done** (sl.) be beaten up **fuckin'** (vulg.) slang expression of extreme annoyance **to bully** ['bʊlɪ] threaten, sometimes physically **to swear** curse; use bad language **pathetic** (coll.) h. hopeless

5. Lord of the Flies

"Call me a coward then."

Jack turned to the hunters.

"He's not a hunter. He'd never have got us meat. He isn't a prefect and we don't know anything about him. He just gives orders and expects people to obey for nothing. All this talk –"

"All this talk!" shouted Ralph. "Talk, talk! Who wanted it? Who called the meeting?"

Jack turned, red in the face, his chin sunk back. He glowered up under his eyebrows.

"All right then," he said in tones of deep meaning, and menace, "all right."

He held the conch against his chest with one hand and stabbed the air with his index finger.

"Who thinks Ralph oughtn't to be chief?"

He looked expectantly at the boys ranged round, who had frozen. Under the palms there was deadly silence.

"Hands up," said Jack strongly, "whoever wants Ralph not to be chief?"

The silence continued, breathless and heavy and full of shame. Slowly the red drained from Jack's cheeks, then came back with a painful rush. He licked his lips and turned his head at an angle, so that his gaze avoided the embarrassment of linking with another's eye.

"How many think –"

His voice tailed off. The hands that held the conch shook. He cleared his throat, and spoke loudly.

"All right then."

He laid the conch with great care in the grass at his feet. The humiliating tears were running from the corner of each eye.

"I'm not going to play any longer. Not with you."

Most of the boys were looking down now, at the grass or their feet. Jack cleared his throat again.

"I'm not going to be part of Ralph's lot –"

He looked along the right-hand logs, numbering the hunters that had been a choir.

"I'm going off by myself. He can catch his own pigs. Anyone who wants to hunt when I do can come too."

He blundered out of the triangle towards the drop to the white sand.

"Jack!"

Jack turned and looked back at Ralph. For a moment he paused and then cried out, high-pitched, enraged.

"– No!"

He leapt down from the platform and ran along the beach, paying no heed to the steady fall of his tears; and until he dived into the forest Ralph watched him.

William Golding (1954)

coward s.o. afraid of danger, hardship, or pain **prefect** in British schools one of a number of senior pupils given responsibility for keeping order **to obey** do what one is told to do **to glower** ['glaʊə] look in an angry or threatening way **menace** ['menəs] threat **conch** large spiral shell **index finger** forefinger **(to be) ranged round** placed or arranged in a circle **to drain** h. disappear **rush** rapid movement **embarrassment** feeling of discomfort; G. Verlegenheit **to tail off** disappear gradually **to humiliate** lower the dignity or self-respect of **lot** (coll.) group **log** tree trunk that has been cut down **choir** ['kwaɪə] group of people trained to sing together **to blunder** h. move uncertainly, as if blind **drop** steep, almost vertical slope **high-pitched** shrill **enraged** very angry **to pay heed to** pay attention to

6. Zigger Zagger

Scene two

Harry Philton – his life.

Zigger: Harry Philton – this is his life.

Enter Policeman, Dentist, Headmaster, Caretaker, Teacher *and* Newsagent.

Policeman: Harry Philton? Yes. Let me see. Is he one of them in the blocks? Ye-es. Well, he'll be just like the rest of them.

Dentist: I'm Harry Philton's school dentist. He's just like the rest of them. Too many sweets. When he's thirty he'll have a mouth full of gums.

HEADMASTER: I'm Harry Philton's Headmaster. He's just like the rest of them. Stupid. If he'd left school when he was twelve, he'd have left knowing as much as he does now. Besides, he chews the ends off the pencils.

CARETAKER: I'm the caretaker of Harry Philton's school. Do you want my opinion of the whole lot of 'em? It's the free milk. I wouldn't give them free milk. And I know. It's only the likes of me knows what they do with the dirty straws.

TEACHER: I'm Harry Philton's class teacher. When he was eleven he could add fractions but not do decimals. Now he's fifteen he's doing decimals but he's forgotten fractions. I would say that if he has to hold two ideas in his head at the same time, it's a severe case of overcrowding. He drills holes in the protractors with the compasses and I know I can't prove it, but I think he pinches the rubbers.

[*Exit everybody except* NEWSAGENT.]

NEWSAGENT: Don't listen to those fellers. Dentists, teachers, social workers. They don't know. Load of old cobblers. I'm the newsagent round here and Harry does a round for me. He's in here at five in the morning, delivers till school time, goes to school to sleep it off, back here at five at night, finished at eight. Gets all of nineteen bob a week. Of course, this is a family man's district so I do a good round in spiceys. I've got a well-thumbed pornography rack. Look at this lot, forty-five cents, all American.

Peter Terson (1970)

caretaker person paid to look after a house, school, shop, etc. **newsagent** seller of newspapers, magazines, etc. **block** tall and large building with lots of flats in it **gum** G. Zahnfleisch **to chew** bite **lot** (coll.) group **the likes of me** (coll.) people like myself **fraction** (math.) G. Bruch **decimal** G. Dezimalzahl **protractor** instrument for measuring and drawing angles **compasses** ['kʌmpəsɪz] instrument used for drawing circles **to pinch** (coll.) steal **feller** (coll.) fellow **load of old cobblers** (sl.) what a lot of rubbish **to do a round** h. deliver newspapers and magazines in a certain district **bob** former British coin, called *shilling* (replaced by the 5p coin) **spicey** h. pornographic magazine **well-thumbed** worn by frequent reading **rack** shelf **lot** h. selection

7. A Christmas Carol

No warmth could warm, no wintry weather chill him. No wind that blew was bitterer than he, no falling snow was more intent upon its purpose, no pelting rain less open to entreaty. Foul weather didn't know where to have him. The heaviest rain, and snow, and hail, and sleet, could boast of the advantage over him in only one respect. They often 'came down' handsomely, and Scrooge never did.

Nobody ever stopped him in the street to say, with gladsome looks, 'My dear Scrooge, how are you? When will you come to see me?' No beggars implored him to bestow a trifle, no children asked him what it was o'clock, no man or woman ever once in all his life inquired the way to such and such a place, of Scrooge. Even the blind men's dogs appeared to know him; and when they saw him coming on, would tug their owners into doorways and up courts; and then would wag their tails as though they said, 'No eye at all is better than an evil eye, dark master!'

But what did Scrooge care! It was the very thing he liked. To edge his way along the crowded paths of life, warning all human sympathy to keep its distance, was what the knowing ones call 'nuts' to Scrooge.

Charles Dickens (1843)

to chill make s.o. feel cold or unpleasant **to be intent upon** aim at directly **to pelt** rain very heavily **entreaty** earnest request **to have s.o.** get s.o. **hail** G. Hagel **sleet** G. Schneeregen **to boast** h. praise s.o. **gladsome** (obs.) glad **to implore** ask earnestly for **to bestow** [bɪˈstəʊ] give as a gift **trifle** s.th. very small or unimportant **to tug** pull energetically **court** yard **to wag** move from side to side **nuts** (coll.) h. pleasure

8.

. . . SO YOU THINK YOU COULD SELL ?

Selling Classified advertisement space on the telephone is a difficult job Selling for The Observer, Britain's oldest Sunday newspaper, is particularly demanding Our standards are very high and only exceptional people are likely to succeed with us

But, if you are aged 21-27 yrs., are intelligent, articulate and quick thinking you may be one of the people we are looking for to join our young, dynamic team this Autumn You will be certain of your ability to work consistently hard under pressure in a fast moving environment, where results are everything Above all you will be positive, determined and confident in your capacity to deal with business people at all levels

If you can demonstrate these qualities we will train you to become a professional salesperson

You will earn £7,399.60 p.a., rising to £7,738.12 p.a (after successfully completing two months service) plus up to £40 per week in bonus on achieving sales targets. You will enjoy five weeks holiday a year, (rising to six weeks after one year's service).

Once you are a member of our impressive team your progress will be linked directly to your own ability, commitment and results.

To apply telephone
Jess Watts
on
01-248 3495

THE OBSERVER

The Observer, 16 September 1984

classified advertisements advertisements arranged in certain classes or groups (e.g. jobs, housing) **demanding** requiring a great deal of skill and ability **exceptional** talented and extremely clever **articulate** able to put thoughts and feelings into clear speech **consistently** (adv.) constantly **capacity** ability **p.a.** *per annum*, in a year **target** total which is desired to be reached **commitment** complete concentration on a task **to apply** ask for a job

9. Saturday Afternoon

Tom Denny shoved the hunk of meat out of his way and stretched out on the meat block. He wanted to lie on his back and rest. The meat block was the only comfortable place in the butcher shop where a man could stretch out and Tom just had to rest every once in a while. He could prop his foot on the edge of the block, swing the other leg across his knee and be fairly comfortable with a hunk of rump steak under his head. The meat was nice and cool just after it came from the icehouse. Tom did that. He wanted to rest himself a while and he had to be comfortable on the meat block. He kicked off his shoes so he could wiggle his toes.

Tom's butcher shop did not have a very pleasant smell. Strangers who went in to buy Tom's meat for the first time were always asking him what it was that had died between the walls. The smell got worse and worse year after year.

Tom bit off a chew of tobacco and made himself comfortable on the meat block.

There was a swarm of flies buzzing around the place; those lazy, stinging, fat and greasy flies that lived in Tom's butcher shop. A screen door at the front kept out some of them that tried to get inside, but if they were used to coming in and filling up on the fresh blood on the meat block they knew how to fly around to the back door where there had never been a screen.

Everybody ate Tom's meat, and liked it. There was no other butcher shop in town. You walked in and said, "Hello, Tom. How's everything today?" "Everything's slick as a whistle with me, but my old woman's got the chills and fever again." Then after Tom had finished telling how it felt to have chills and fever, you said, "I want a pound of pork chops, Tom." And Tom said, "By gosh, I'll git it for you right away." While you stood around waiting for the chops Tom turned the hunk of beef over two or three times businesslike and hacked off a pound of pork for you. If you wanted veal it was all the same to Tom. He slammed the hunk of beef around several times making a great to-do, and got the veal for you. He pleased everybody. Ask Tom for any kind of meat you could name, and Tom had it right there on the meat block waiting to be cut off and weighed.

Tom brushed the flies off his face and took a little snooze. It was midday. The country people had not yet got to town. It was laying-by season and everybody was working right up to twelve o'clock sun time, which was half an hour slower than railroad time. There was hardly anybody in town at this time of day, even though it was Saturday. All the town people who had wanted some of Tom's meat for Saturday dinner had already got what they needed, and it was too early in the day to buy Sunday meat. The best time of day to get meat from Tom if it was to be kept over until Sunday was about ten o'clock Saturday night. Then you could take it home and be fairly certain that it would not turn bad before noon the next day – if the weather was not too hot.

The flies buzzed and lit on Tom's mouth and nose and Tom knocked them away with his hand and tried to sleep on the meat block with the cool hunk of rump steak under his head. The tobacco juice kept trying to trickle down his throat and Tom had to keep spitting it out. There was a cigar box half full of sawdust in the corner behind the showcase where livers and brains were kept for display, but he could not quite spit that far from the position he was in. The tobacco juice splattered on the floor midway between the meat block and cigar box. What little of it dripped on the piece of rump steak did not really matter: most people cleaned their meat before they cooked and ate it, and it would all wash off.

But the danged flies! They kept on buzzing and stinging as mean as ever, and there is nothing any meaner than a lazy, well-fed, butcher-shop fly in the summertime, anyway, Tom knocked them off his face and spat them off his mouth the best he could without having to move too much. After a while he let them alone.

Tom was enjoying a good little snooze when Jim Baxter came running through the back door from the barbershop on the corner. Jim was Tom's partner and he came in sometimes on busy days to help out. He was a great big man, almost twice as large as Tom. He always wore a big wide-brimmed black hat and a blue shirt with the sleeves rolled up above his elbows. He had a large egg-shaped belly over which his breeches were always slipping down. When he walked he tugged at his breeches all the time, pulling them up over the top of his belly. But they were always working down until it looked as if they were ready to drop to the ground any minute and trip him. Jim would not wear suspenders. A belt was more sporty-looking.

Tom was snoozing away when Jim ran in the back door and grabbed him by the shoulders. A big handful of flies had gone to sleep on Tom's mouth. Jim shooed them off.

"Hey, Tom, Tom!" Jim shouted breathlessly. "Wake up, Tom! Wake up quick!"

Tom jumped to the floor and pulled on his shoes. He had become so accustomed to people coming in and waking him up to buy a quarter's worth of steak or a quarter's worth of ham that he had mistaken Jim for a customer. He rubbed the back of his hands over his mouth to take away the fly stings.

"What the hell!" he sputtered, looking up and seeing Jim standing there beside him. "What you want?"

"Come on, Tom! Git your gun! We're going after a nigger down the creek a ways."

"God Almighty, Jim!" Tom shouted, now fully awake. He clutched Jim's arm and begged: "You going to git a nigger, sure enough?"

"You're damn right, Tom. You know that gingerbread nigger what used to work on the railroad a long time back? Him's the nigger we're going to git. And we're going to git him good and proper, the yellow-face coon. He said something to Fred Jackson's oldest gal down the road yonder about an hour ago. Fred told us all about it over at the barber-shop. Come on, Tom. We got to hurry. I expect we'll jerk him up pretty soon now."

Tom tied on his shoes and ran across the street behind Jim. Tom had his shotgun under his arm, and Jim had pulled the cleaver out of the meat block. They'd get the God-damn nigger all right – God damn his yellow hide to hell!

Tom climbed into an automobile with some other men. Jim jumped on the running board of another car just as it was leaving. There were thirty or forty cars headed for the creek bottom already and more getting ready to start.

They had a place already picked out at the creek. There was a clearing in the woods by the road and there was just enough room to do the job like it should be done. Plenty of dry brushwood nearby and a good-sized sweetgum tree in the middle of the clearing. The automobiles stopped and the men jumped out in a hurry. Some others had gone for Will Maxie. Will was the gingerbread Negro. They would probably find him at home laying his cotton by. Will could grow good cotton. He cut out all the grass first, and then he banked his rows with earth. Everybody else laid his cotton by without going to the trouble of taking out the grass. But Will was a pretty smart Negro. And he could raise a lot of corn too, to the acre. He always cut out the grass before he laid his corn by. But nobody liked Will. He made too much money by taking out the grass before laying by his cotton and corn. He made more money than Tom and Jim made in the butcher shop selling people meat.

Doc Cromer had sent his boy down from the drugstore with half a dozen cases of Coca-Cola and a piece of ice in a wash tub. The tub had some muddy water put in it from the creek, then the chunk of ice, and then three cases of Coca-Cola. When they were gone the boy would put the other three cases in the tub and give the dopes a chance to cool. Everybody likes to drink a lot of dopes when they are nice and cold.

Tom went out in the woods to take a drink of corn with Jim and Hubert Wells. Hubert always carried a jug of corn with him wherever he happened to be going. He made the whisky himself at his own still and got a fairly good living by selling it around the courthouse and the barbershop. Hubert made the best corn in the county.

Will Maxie was coming up the big road in a hurry. A couple of dozen men were behind him poking him with sticks. Will was getting old. He had a wife and three grown daughters, all married and settled. Will was a pretty good Negro too, minding his own business, stepping out of the road when he met a white man, and otherwise behaving himself. But nobody liked Will. He made too much money by taking the grass out of his cotton before it was laid by.

Will came running up the road and the men steered him into the clearing. It was all fixed. There was a big pile of brushwood and a trace chain for his neck and one for his feet. That would hold him. There were two or three cans of gasoline, too.

Doc Cromer's boy was doing a good business with his Coca-Colas. Only five or six bottles of the first three cases were left in the wash tub. He was getting ready to put the other cases in now and give the dopes a chance to get nice and cool. Everybody likes to have a dope every once in a while.

The Cromer boy would probably sell out and have to go back to town and bring back several more cases. And yet there was not such a big crowd today, either. It was the hot weather that made people have to drink a lot of dopes to stay cool. There were only a hundred and fifty or seventy-five there today. There had not been enough time for the word to get passed around. Tom would have missed it if Jim had not run in and told him about it while he was taking a nap on the meat block.

Will Maxie did not drink Coca-Cola. Will never spent his money on anything like that. That was what was wrong with him. He was too damn good for a Negro. He did not drink corn whisky, nor make it; he did not carry a knife, nor a razor; he bared his head when he met a white man, and he lived with his own wife. But they had him now! God damn his gingerbread hide to hell! They had him where he could not take any more grass out of his cotton before laying it by. They had him tied to a sweet-gum tree in the clearing at the creek with a trace chain around his neck and another around his knees. Yes, sir, they had Will Maxie now, the yellow-face coon! He would not take any more grass out of his cotton before laying it by!

Tom was feeling good. Hubert gave him another drink in the woods. Hubert was all right. He made good corn whisky. Tom liked him for that. And Hubert always took his wife a big piece of meat Saturday night to use over Sunday. Nice meat, too. Tom cut off the meat and Hubert took it home and made a present of it to his wife.

Will Maxie was going up in smoke. When he was just about gone they gave him the lead. Tom stood back and took good aim and fired away at Will with his shotgun as fast as he could breech it and put in a new load. About forty or more of the other men had shotguns too. They filled him so full of lead that his body sagged from his neck where the trace chain held him up.

The Cromer boy had sold completely out. All of his ice and dopes were gone. Doc Cromer would feel pretty good when his boy brought back all that money. Six whole cases he sold, at a dime a bottle. If he had brought along another case or two he could have sold them easily enough. Everybody likes Coca-Cola. There is nothing better to drink on a hot day, if the dopes are nice and cool.

After a while the men got ready to draw the body up in the tree and tie it to a limb so it could hang there, but Tom and Jim could not wait and they went back to town the first chance they got to ride. They were in a big hurry. They had been gone several hours and it was almost four o'clock. A lot of people came downtown early Saturday afternoon to get their Sunday meat before it was picked over by the country people. Tom and Jim had to hurry back and open up the meat market and get to work slicing steaks and chopping soupbones with the cleaver on the meat block. Tom was the butcher. He did all the work with the meat. He went out and killed a cow and quartered her. Then he hauled the meat to the butcher shop and hung it on the hooks in the icehouse. When somebody wanted to buy some meat, he took one of the quarters from the hook and threw it on the meat block and cut what you asked for. You told Tom what you wanted and he gave it to you, no matter what it was you asked for.

Then you stepped over to the counter and paid Jim the money for it. Jim was the cashier. He did all the talking, too. Tom had to do the cutting and weighing. Jim's egg-shaped belly was too big for him to work around the meat block. It got in his way when he tried to slice you a piece of tenderloin steak, so Tom did that and Jim took the money and put it into the cashbox under the counter.

Tom and Jim got back to town just in time. There was a big crowd standing around on the street getting ready to do their weekly trading, and they had to have some meat. You went in the butcher shop and said,

"Hello, Tom. I want two pounds and a half of pork chops." Tom said, "Hello, I'll get it for you right away." While you were waiting for Tom to cut the meat off the hunk of rump steak you asked him how was everything.

"Everything's slick as a whistle," he said, "except my old woman's got the chills and fever pretty bad again."

Tom weighed the pork chops and wrapped them up for you and then you stepped over to Jim and paid him the money. Jim was the cashier. His egg-shaped belly was too big for him to work around the meat block. Tom did that part, and Jim took the money and put it into the cashbox under the counter.

Erskine Caldwell (1941)

to shove [ʃʌv] push **hunk** large piece **to prop** lean against a support **to wiggle** move with quick, short, side-to-side movements **chew of tobacco** piece of chewing tobacco **to sting** [stɪŋ] (often insect) prick or bite **greasy** oily **screen door** door consisting of a frame and fine wire netting to keep out flies **slick as a whistle** (sl.) excellent, fine **chills and fever** malaria **chop** thick slice of meat with bone in it **by gosh** (sl.) by God **git** get **veal** meat of a calf **to slam** h. turn with force and noise **to make a great to-do** G. viel Aufhebens machen **snooze** short sleep **laying-by season** harvest season **to (a) light (lit, lit)** land **sawdust** G. Sägemehl **showcase** case with glass sides and top for showing and protecting articles in a shop **display** showing **to splatter** splash **danged** [dæŋd] damned **mean** nasty, bad **barbershop** hairdresser's shop **wide-brimmed** G. breitkrempig **belly** stomach **breeches** trousers **to tug** pull **to trip** make s.o. stumble **suspenders** G. Hosenträger **a quarter** 25 cents **to sputter** to stammer **creek** very small river **to clutch** seize or grasp firmly **you going** you are going **gingerbread** G. Ingwerbrot; h. referring to the colour of skin **what used** who used **him's** he's **yellow-face** cowardly **coon** (pej.) negro **gal** girl **yonder** over there **to jerk s.o. up** (sl.) hang **cleaver** heavy long-bladed knife **hide** skin **running board** G. Trittbrett **bottom** source of a river **clearing** open space in a forest **brushwood** undergrowth **to bank** cover **smart** clever, bright **to the acre** per acre **drugstore** shop where a wide variety of articles are sold and where medicines can be collected **case** box **tub** open container with a flat bottom **chunk** big lump **dope** cola drink **corn** corn whisky **jug** G. Krug **still** distillery **courthouse** public building in which courts of law are held **to poke** push **settled** provided for **to mind one's own business** not to interfere in the affairs of others **to steer** direct with some force **trace chain** G. Fessel **gasoline** petrol **nap** short sleep **razor** G. Rasierklinge **to bare one's head** take one's hat off **to go up in smoke** be burnt completely **to give s.o. the lead** shoot s.o. **to breech** open a shotgun **to sag** sink or bend down under weight **dime** U.S. coin worth ten cents **limb** [lɪm] strong branch (of a tree) **to ride** be taken in a vehicle **to pick over** examine and choose **to haul** pull with effort or force **tenderloin** G. zartes Lendenstück

Chapter V

Stylistic Devices

Introductory Remarks

The original and principal aim of communication, in whatever form, is to pass on a message clearly and accurately without any confusion, ambiguity, or misunderstanding. The language used in this context sticks as closely as possible to the conventional meaning of words. However, as soon as one employs additional stylistic devices to increase or broaden meaning, to exaggerate, understate, or manipulate, to entertain, or provide aesthetic pleasure one deviates from the basic convention. The inclusion of these stylistic devices may confuse or may lead to the reader interpreting them in different ways. In the process a line of argumentation may be lost, a viewpoint may be misinterpreted, different readers may translate these rhetorical signals differently. In other words, the greater the density of stylistic devices in a text, the greater the likelihood of this text being understood and appreciated in a number of ways.

The meaning of a text can also be modified by what is often called *tone*, i.e. the expression of the speaker's attitudes towards a text's subject, towards its readers, and towards himself or herself. Irony, sarcasm, humour, anger, polemic are just some of the kinds of tone which can be conveyed in a text. The manipulative effect of point of view on the reader should be mentioned here, too. (See chapter III for comprehensive details).

To facilitate access to a notoriously difficult field in text analysis the large number of stylistic devices has been reduced to those most frequently employed; they are grouped together in the following table according to their general functions of *repetition/variation, contrast,* and *imagery/analogy* and according to their location in a text (lexical or word level; syntactical or sentence level; compositional or text level). A word of warning: It is not enough to simply spot a stylistic device and then mention your discovery. You must pursue your detective work further in order to work out why that particular device is used in that particular context and to judge its effect and appropriateness.

Repetition/Variation

alliteration	recurrence of initial sound
accumulation	series of expressions that contribute increasingly to meaning
parallelism	repetition of syntactical structures, (sub-)clauses, (parts of) sentences
anaphora	[ə'næfərə] repetition of first word(s) of lines/clauses
leitmotif	a dominant recurrent theme (word, phrase, emotion, idea) associated with a certain idea, person, or situation and accompanying its/his/her reappearance throughout the text
climax	the point of highest dramatic tension or a major turning point in the action of a text

Contrast

euphemism	[juːfɪmɪzm] stylistic device intended to hide the real nature of s.th. unpleasant or taboo by using a mild or indirect expression
oxymoron	[- -'- -] combination of two terms which are contradictory in meaning; e.g. "eloquent silence"
paradox	seemingly self-contradictory or absurd statement which in fact establishes a more complex level of meaning by way of association; e.g. "I see it feelingly."
antithesis	a rhetorical figure which denotes the opposing of ideas by means of grammatically parallel arrangements of words, clauses, or sentences
anti-climax	a sudden transition from an idea of significance or dignity to an idea trivial or ludicrous by comparison
rhetorical question	an assertion in the form of a question which strongly suggests a particular response
antithesis (comp.)	the second of two opposing ideas developed at length in a text
anti-climax (comp.)	a sudden shift of extended ideas, events, or situations from the significant to the trivial

Imagery/Analogy

onomatopoeia	[ˌɒnəʊmætəʊˈpiːə] sound(s) imitative of thing(s) they refer to
metaphor	[ˈmetəfə] a reduced or implied comparison between phenomena not normally associated with each other
symbol	denotes a concrete thing that stands for s.th. immaterial or abstract
connotation	this term implies additional meaning(s) of a word or phrase along with or apart from what it explicitly names or describes
metonymy	[-'- - -] the object meant is not explicitly named but rather substituted by a closely associated feature, a characteristic part, or a proper name
personification	figure of speech in which inanimate objects, abstract concepts or living things (plants, animals) are referred to as if they were human beings
pun	a humorous play on words which are either identical or similar in sound but are very different in meaning
simile	an explicit comparison (using *as* or *like*) between two distinctly different things which have at least one feature in common
example	this device serves to illustrate an abstract rule, or acts as an exercise in the application of this rule; (can also be a single fact, item, or incident)

	lexical	**syntactical**	**compositional**
repetition/ variation	alliteration	accumulation parallelism anaphora	leitmotif climax
contrast	euphemism oxymoron	paradox antithesis anti-climax rhetorical question	antithesis anti-climax
imagery/ analogy	onomatopoeia metaphor symbol connotation metonymy personification pun	simile	example

Of course this table of technical terms is by no means exhaustive. The rules of usefulness and frequency determined the selection. This grouping into relevant sections complements the definitions given above and is meant to add to their clarity.

1. Give a short summary of each text.
2. Identify and describe the stylistic devices in the text and explain their functions. Do these devices, in your opinion, serve the text's purpose?
3. Find a text from your own reading containing stylistic devices discussed in this chapter.
4. Creative writing: write your own text (e.g. advertisement, speech, debate) using stylistic devices where useful.

Points for discussion: Human Rights and Democracy
War and Heroism
Religion and Faith
Attitudes to Education
Creativity

Useful Phrases

1. to	use	figures of speech
	employ	stylistic devices

2. The author	uses	metaphorical language.
	resorts to	

3. The stylistic device	enhances	the argument of the text.
	underscores	

4. to employ	visual	devices
	tactile	
	auditive	

5. to	describe	s.th. by	a metaphor
	depict		a symbol
			metonymy
			allegory
			...

6. The text	abounds in	stylistic devices.
	contains	

7. to	draw	a(n)	analogy
	set up		symmetry
	create		parallelism
			leitmotif
			...

8. This passage contains	many	stylistic devices.
	few	

9. to	examine	the dominant stylistic devices
	explain	
	analyse	
	uncover	

10. to	make	a	comparison	between
	form		simile	

11. The style of the text is	condensed
	plain
	vivid
	banal
	pompous
	artificial
	long-winded

12. The stylistic device	affirms	the author's message.
	supports	

13. a symbol	represents	(shades of) meaning
	expresses	
	signifies	

14. The text is	organised	according to certain patterns
	structured	

15. to	comment on	the	significance	of a stylistic device
	reveal		meaning	
			impact	

16. words	constitute the	compositional	patterns of the text
sentences		structural	
paragraphs			

17. a stylistic device	brings out	additional significance
	creates	

18. the use of stylistic devices achieves	positive	effects on the reader
	negative	
	impressive	
	contradictory	
	polemical	

19. stylistic devices establish	a	climactic	text structure
	an	anti-climactic	
		antithetical	

20. a stylistic device	strengthens	the main arguments of the text
	focuses on	

21. to discuss the function of a stylistic device

22. The text	is devoid of	stylistic devices
	lacks	

23. Certain stylistic devices are employed	repeatedly
	often
	only once

1. The Declaration of Independence 1776

We hold these truths to be self-evident, that all men are created equal, that they are endowed by their Creator with certain unalienable Rights, that among these are Life, Liberty and the pursuit of Happiness.

That to secure these rights, Governments are instituted among Men, deriving their just powers from the consent of the governed, That whenever any Form of Government becomes destructive of these ends, it is the Right of the People to alter or to abolish it, and to institute a new Government, laying its foundation on such principles, and organizing its powers in such form, as to them shall seem most likely to effect their Safety and Happiness. Prudence, indeed, will dictate that Governments long established should not be changed for light and transient causes; and accordingly all experience hath shown, that mankind are more disposed to suffer, while evils are sufferable, than to right themselves by abolishing the forms to which they are accustomed.

2. The Constitution of the United States of America 1787

We the People of the United States, in Order to form a more perfect Union, establish Justice, insure domestic Tranquility, provide for the common defense, promote the general Welfare, and secure the Blessings of Liberty to ourselves and our Posterity, do ordain and establish this Constitution for the United States of America.

self-evident clear without need of proof **to be endowed with** be born with **unalienable** which cannot be taken away **pursuit of** striving after **to derive** get **just** right and fair **consent** agreement **to abolish** get rid of **to effect** bring about **prudence** wisdom **transient** ['trænzɪənt] for a short time only; temporary **hath** (obs.) has **disposed** ready, willing **to right o.s.** bring about justice for o.s. **domestic** h. of o.'s own country **tranquility** calmness and peace **to promote** encourage **welfare** well-being; comfort and happiness **blessing** h. advantage; gift **posterity** future generations **to ordain** set up a law

3. An Irish Airman foresees his Death

I KNOW that I shall meet my fate
Somewhere among the clouds above;
Those that I fight I do not hate,
Those that I guard I do not love;
My country is Kiltartan Cross,
My countrymen Kiltartan's poor,
No likely end could bring them loss
Or leave them happier than before.
Nor law, nor duty bade me fight,
Nor public men, nor cheering crowds,
A lonely impulse of delight
Drove to this tumult in the clouds;
I balanced all, brought all to mind,
The years to come seemed waste of breath,
A waste of breath the years behind
In balance with this life, this death.

William Butler Yeats (1865–1939)

fate h. death **to guard** protect; keep from danger **Kiltartan Cross** region round the village of Kiltartan in the county of Galway, Ireland **likely** expected; probable **bade** [bæd;beɪd] (past form of bid) command; ask to do s.th. **tumult** ['tju:mʌlt]

4. The Creation of the World

IN THE BEGINNING OF CREATION, when God made heaven and earth, the earth was without form and void, with darkness over the face of the abyss, and a mighty wind that swept over the surface of the waters. God said, 'Let there be light', and there was light; and God saw that the light was good, and he separated light from darkness. He called the light day, and the darkness night. So evening came, and morning came, the first day.

God said, 'Let there be a vault between the waters, to separate water from water.' So God made the vault, and separated the water under the vault from the water above it, and so it was; and God called the vault heaven. Evening came, and morning came, a second day.

God said, 'Let the waters under heaven be gathered into one place, so that dry land may appear'; and so it was. God called the dry land earth, and the gathering of the waters he called seas; and God saw that it was good. Then God said, 'Let the earth produce fresh growth, let there be on the earth plants bearing seed, fruit-trees bearing fruit each with seed according to its kind.' So it was; the earth yielded fresh growth, plants bearing seed according to their kind and trees bearing fruit each with seed according to its kind; and God saw that it was good. Evening came, and morning came, a third day.

From *The Book of Genesis*

void empty **abyss** ['- -] hole so deep as to appear bottomless **vault** G. Wölbung **seed** part of a flowering plant from which another plant can grow; G. Same **to yield** produce; give s.th. as a result

5. Anthem for Doomed Youth

What passing-bells for these who die as cattle?
   Only the monstrous anger of the guns.
   Only the stuttering rifles' rapid rattle
Can patter out their hasty orisons.
No mockeries now for them; no prayers nor bells,
   Nor any voice of mourning save the choirs, –
The shrill, demented choirs of wailing shells;
   And bugles calling for them from sad shires.

What candles may be held to speed them all?
   Not in the hands of boys, but in their eyes
Shall shine the holy glimmers of good-byes.
   The pallor of girls' brows shall be their pall;
Their flowers the tenderness of patient minds,
And each slow dusk a drawing-down of blinds.

Wilfred Owen (1893–1918)

anthem church hymn or the official song of a nation **doomed** not in a position to avoid death; G. dem Untergang geweiht **passing-bell** bell rung at the moment of a person's death **stuttering** h. rapidly repeating the same sound **orison** ['ɒrɪzn] prayer **save** except **choir** ['kwaɪə] group of people trained to sing together **demented** mad-sounding **to wail** make a sad, usually shrill, crying sound **shell** G. Granate **bugle** [bju:gl] sort of trumpet used for military signals and ceremonies **shire** county **pallor** paleness, whiteness, esp. of the face **pall** [pɔ:l] heavy cloth spread over a coffin at a funeral **dusk** time in the evening just before it gets quite dark **blind** roll of cloth fixed on a roller and pulled down to cover a window

6.

MYTH

"The GLC is a reckless spender, unable to control its own expenditure compared to Central Government."

FACT

"During the period 1978/79 to 1983/84 current expenditure on goods and services administered directly by Central Government increased by 101%. Over the same period GLC gross revenue expenditure increased by 88%."

MYTH

"Abolishing the GLC will save millions of pounds and cut down bureaucracy."

FACT

"It must be inevitable that it will cost more to run and administer the GLC's many functions by setting up quangos and boards and forcing already hard-pressed London Boroughs to take on even more. GLC administrative and managerial staff amount to only 7½% of total staff and their wage bill is 2% of the GLC's total cost. Over half the GLC staff are fire fighters or public health and safety workers."

MYTH

"London doesn't need the GLC – look at other capital cities."

FACT

"If the GLC were to be abolished then London would be the only capital city in the western world without a democratically elected strategic local authority."

Keep GLC
Working for London

New Statesman, 14 October 1983

myth s.th. that is invented **GLC** Greater London Council (now abolished) **reckless** not thinking of the consequences **expenditure** spending **to abolish** put an end to; do away with **current** h. fixed **to administer** [-'---] control; manage **gross revenue** ['revɪnju:] total (annual) income **inevitable** [-'----] sure to happen **quango** quasi-autonomous non-governmental organization; partly independent official committee **board** committee **hard-pressed** h. short of money **Borough** ['bʌrə] **staff** people working under the same manager **wage** hourly-paid earnings; G. Lohn

7. Little by Little

Little by little, the fight against cancer is being won.

Hodgkin's disease was once an almost certain killer.

Today the recovery rate for children is 90%.

Fifteen years ago there was no effective treatment for Leukaemia.

Today 50% of children survive, and we believe that it will soon be more.

Twenty years ago there were two or three active anti-cancer drugs.

Today there are between 30 and 40.

The Observer, 2 October 1983

cancer G. Krebs **Hodgkin's disease** a chronic infectious disease with effects similar to those of leukaemia **recovery rate** number of people cured **leukaemia** [lju:'ki:mɪə]

8. Julius Caesar

Antony. Friends, Romans, countrymen, lend me your ears;
I come to bury Caesar, not to praise him.
The evil that men do lives after them,
The good is oft interred with their bones;
So let it be with Caesar. The noble Brutus
Hath told you Caesar was ambitious.
If it were so, it was a grievous fault,
And grievously hath Caesar answer'd it.

Here, under leave of Brutus and the rest,
(For Brutus is an honourable man,
So are they all, all honourable men)
Come I to speak in Caesar's funeral.
He was my friend, faithful and just to me;
But Brutus says he was ambitious,
And Brutus is an honourable man.
He hath brought many captives home to Rome,
Whose ransoms did the general coffers fill:
Did this in Caesar seem ambitious?
When that the poor have cried, Caesar hath wept;
Ambition should be made of sterner stuff:
Yet Brutus says he was ambitious,
And Brutus is an honourable man.
You all did see that on the Lupercal
I thrice presented him a kingly crown,
Which he did thrice refuse. Was this ambition?
Yet Brutus says he was ambitious,
And sure he is an honourable man.
I speak not to disprove what Brutus spoke,
But here I am to speak what I do know.

William Shakespeare, *Julius Caesar* III, 2, 75–103

to inter [in'tɜː] bury **hath** (obs.) has **ambitious** having a strong desire for success, fame, power, wealth, etc. **grievous** severe **under leave** with permission, consent **just** fair; in accordance with what is right **captive** person taken prisoner **ransom** sum of money paid to free a captive **coffers** (pl.) place for storing valuables, esp. money **to be made of stern stuff** be a tough and hard person **Lupercal** cave on Palatine hill in ancient Rome, sacred to Lupercus, connected with the story of Romulus and Remus **thrice** three times **to disprove** show to be wrong or false

9. Another Brick in the Wall, part 2

We don't need no education
We don't need no thought control
No dark sarcasm in the classroom
Teachers leave the kids alone
Hey teacher leave us kids alone
All in all it's just another brick in the wall
All in all you're just another brick in the wall

Pink Floyd, *The Wall* (1979)

brick man-made stone used for building **don't need no** (sl.) need no; don't need any **sarcasm** speaking or writing which tries to hurt s.o.'s feelings, esp. by expressions which clearly mean the opposite of what is felt

10. Miscellaneous

a) An aged man is but a paltry thing,
A tattered coat upon a stick...

W. B. Yeats, *Sailing to Byzantium*

*

b) Motto at a dietetic food store: If you are thin, don't eat fast. If you are fat, don't eat: fast.

*

c) A bachelor girl was asked the perennial question – why she hadn't married. She replied, "I could marry anyone I please; but so far I haven't found anyone I please."

*

d) At the drunkard's funeral four of his friends carried the bier.

*

e) MERCUTIO: I am hurt,
A plague o' both your houses. I am sped.
Is he gone, and hath nothing?
BENVOLIO: What, art thou hurt?
MERCUTIO: Ay, ay, a scratch, a scratch. Marry, 'tis enough.
Where is my page? Go villain, fetch a surgeon.
[*Exit Page.*]
ROMEO: Courage, man, the hurt cannot be much.
MERCUTIO: No, 'tis not so deep as a well, nor so wide as a church door, but 'tis enough, 'twill serve. Ask for me tomorrow and you shall find me a grave man.

William Shakespeare, *Romeo and Juliet* III, 1, 91–99

*

f) JUDY: Do you believe in free speech?
PUNCH: I certainly do.
JUDY: Good, can I use your telephone?

*

paltry ['pɔːltrɪ] worthless **tattered** in rags **dietetic** relating to diet and the food to be eaten **fast** quick **to fast** go without food **bachelor** h. unmarried **perennial** always repeated **bier** movable wooden stand for a coffin or a dead body **sped**

(archaic) finished; destroyed **scratch** slight injury (caused by a sharp instrument) **marry** (exclamation of astonishment) **page** servant **villain** rascal; knave; G. Taugenichts **surgeon** doctor who performs operations **well** deep shaft for obtaining water; G. Brunnen **'twill** it will **grave** 1. serious 2. dead

g) **i ron y** ['aiərəni] **n. 1.** [U] the expression of one's meaning by saying sth. which is the direct opposite of one's thoughts, in order to make one's remarks forceful. **2.** [C] event, situation, etc., which is itself desirable, but which, because of the circumstances, is of little or no value, thus appearing to be directed by evil fate: *the ~ of fate (circumstances). If a poor man inherits a large fortune and dies a month later, one might call it one of life's ironies.*

The Advanced Learner's Dictionary of Current English, 2nd ed., Oxford

*

h) The bomb completely destroyed the new cinema, several dozen houses, the cathedral, and my dustbin.

fate events in o.'s life determined in advance **to inherit** receive after s.o.'s death **fortune** h. sum of money

11.

In Memoriam

Hayes in ever loving memory of our darling daughter
Diana Rose who passed away 27 Sept 1969.
In him be thy trust for him thy heart's longing
Mummy Daddy Patricia and Pamela

The Times, 27 September 1983

to pass away die **thy** your

12. The Thought-Fox

I imagine this midnight moment's forest:
Something else is alive
Beside the clock's loneliness
And this blank page where my fingers move.

Through the window I see no star:
Something more near
Though deeper within darkness
Is entering the loneliness:

Cold, delicately as the dark snow
A fox's nose touches twig, leaf;
Two eyes serve a movement, that now
And again now, and now, and now

Sets neat prints into the snow
Between trees, and warily a lame
Shadow lags by stump and in hollow
Of a body that is bold to come

Across clearings, an eye,
A widening deepening greenness,
Brilliantly, concentratedly,
Coming about its own business

Till, with a sudden sharp hot stink of fox
It enters the dark hole of the head.
The window is starless still; the clock ticks,
The page is printed.

Ted Hughes (1930–)

blank with nothing written, printed or drawn on it **delicate** soft **twig** small branch of a tree **to serve** represent **neat** tidy and orderly **print** mark made on a surface, normally a footstep **wary** cautious, careful **lame** h. slow; G. lahm **to lag** move more slowly than others **stump** the remaining part of a tree which has been cut down **hollow** G. Vertiefung **clearing** open space in a forest **to come about o.'s business** usu. go about o.'s business

13. In Church

Often I try
To analyse the quality
Of its silences. Is this where God hides
From my searching? I have stopped to listen,
After the few people have gone,
To the air recomposing itself

For vigil. It has waited like this
Since the stones grouped themselves about it.
These are the hard ribs
Of a body that our prayers have failed
To animate. Shadows advance
From their corners to take possession
Of places the light held
For an hour. The bats resume
Their business. The uneasiness of the pews
Ceases. There is no other sound
In the darkness but the sound of a man
Breathing, testing his faith
On emptiness, nailing his questions
One by one to an untenanted cross.

R. S. Thomas (1913–)

to recompose settle after a disturbance **vigil** staying awake to keep watch or to pray **rib** G. Rippe **to animate** give life to **to advance** come forward **bat** small mouse-like animal that flies at night **to resume** begin again **uneasiness** disturbance **pew** long wooden bench with a back in a church **untenanted** h. empty; **tenant** person with the legal right to use a property

Vater hat geholfen

O. E. Planen. *Vater und Sohn,* re. (Ravensburg: Otto Maier, 1980)

Glossary

This glossary contains the theoretical terms concerned with text analysis which are introduced in this book. The references in brackets behind the entries indicate the respective chapter in which the term is to be found. An asterisk behind a word in one of the glossary explanations signifies that it has an entry of its own in the glossary. As the alphabetical arrangement does not reflect the logical coherence of concepts and entries, this is preceded by a systematic survey of all the entries. Where he, his, himself are used, she, her, herself may also apply.

text:	communication; objectivity; interpretation
text category:	fictional, factional, non-fictional
text form:	**(see chapter I)**
genre:	novel, shorter fiction, drama, poetry
text structure:	introduction/exposition, middle section, final section; composition
text type:	descriptive, narrative, expository, argumentative, instructive
point of view:	*narrator:* telling, showing; omniscient/unlimited point of view; *limited point of view:* central consciousness – reported thought, interior monologue, stream of consciousness –, minor character; eliminated narrator
plot:	setting *character:* round character, flat character; protagonist, conflict; methods of characterisation
stylistic devices:	tone *repetition/variation:* alliteration, accumulation, parallelism, anaphora, leitmotif, climax; *contrast:* euphemism, oxymoron, paradox, antithesis, anti-climax, rhetorical question; *imagery/analogy:* onomatopoeia, metaphor, symbol, connotation, metonymy, personification, pun, simile, example.

accumulation (V) series of expressions belonging to the same semantic field that contribute increasingly to meaning.

alliteration (V) recurrence of initial sound in subsequent words.

anaphora (V) repetition of first word(s) of lines/clauses.

anti-climax (V) a sudden transition from an idea of significance or dignity to an idea trivial or ludicrous by comparison (syntactical level); a sudden shift of extended ideas, events, or situations from the significant to the trivial (compositional level).

antithesis (V) a rhetorical figure which denotes the opposing of ideas by means of grammatically parallel arrangements of words, clauses, or sentences (syntactical level); the second of two opposing ideas developed at length in a text (compositional level).

argumentative text (II) discusses a number of conflicting standpoints in an attempt to evaluate them.

central consciousness (III) the narrator* is the main protagonist* in the story. Everything is seen and evaluated according to its impact and effect on the consciousness of this leading character* through whose eyes the reader follows the course of events. The distance between reader and protagonist can be regulated by presenting the protagonist's psyche in the form of reported thought*, interior monologue* or stream of consciousness*.

character (IV) person presented in a text who is interpreted by the reader as having qualities and attitudes as illustrated by means of dialogue and action or information supplied by the narrator. The main character is called the protagonist*. An important division is that into flat* and round* characters.

climax (V) the point of highest dramatic tension or a major turning point in the action of a text.

communication (introduction/V) the original and principal aim of communication, in whatever form, is to pass on a message clearly and accurately without any confusion, ambiguity, or misunderstanding. Communication comprises four vital parts: *Sender* (author/speaker) – *Message* (intention) – *Code* (text/word) – *Receiver* (reader/listener). *Sender* and *Receiver* include the specific historical, social, economic, and cultural conditions at the time of the text/word production and reception. As the communication between author and receiver via the text is a one way operation, the reader has to find out the meaning of a text by attempting a personal interpretation.

composition (II) arrangement of text sections into introductory/middle/final sections*; the internal composition can be based on the principles of chronology, antithesis, enumeration, symmetry, parallelism; or from the general to the particular, from cause to effect, from preparation to climax* (or vice versa).

conflict (IV) struggle between protagonist* and antagonist as a result of their characteristic features and events. In this conflict the characters* are not important as individuals but as embodiments of fundamental concepts of human experience such as love/hate, life/death, etc.

connotation (V) additional meaning(s) of a word or phrase along with or apart from what it explicitly names or describes (denotation).

contrast (V) group of stylistic devices* based on the principle of opposition, either of expression and meaning, or of two or more contradictory expressions, or of contradictory ideas. To this group belong: euphemism*, oxymoron* (lexical); paradox*, rhetorical question* (syntactical); antithesis*, anti-climax* (syntactical and compositional).

descriptive text (II) makes statements about the physical appearances of people, things, and situations and/or their spatial arrangement.

drama (I) the presentation of the world and characters* through dialogue and gesture. It is principally intended for performance on stage. The basic distinction is that between tragedy and comedy.

eliminated narrator (III) characters*, action, setting*, and events are presented directly without the interference of a narrator*. The characters are depicted through action and speech.

euphemism (V) stylistic device* intended to conceal the real nature of s.th. unpleasant or taboo by using a mild or indirect expression.

example (V) illustration of an abstract rule by reference to concrete events or situations or an exercise in the application of this rule.

expository text (II) sets out to relate concepts, ideas, or opinions in a step-by-step or analytical fashion.

factional text (I) a text with elements of fictional composition and factual reality, the significant feature being the evaluative character.

fictional text (I) a text whose characters* and plot* are invented. Characters, action, and setting* are interrelated and interdependent; they have a specific function in this artificially constructed world which reflects a philosophy of life.

final section (II) it contains the evaluation of a text's preceding ideas, action, and/or description in the forms of an appeal, solution, climax, etc.

flat character (IV) also called type or two-dimensional, i.e. "constructed round a single idea or quality" (E. M. Forster) without much individualising detail or capacity for development.

genre (I) traditional division of texts into prose (novel*, shorter fiction*, etc.), poetry*, and drama*.

imagery/analogy (V) group of stylistic devices based on the overt or hidden similarity of sounds, words, or ideas/concepts expressed in direct or implicit comparisons. This group includes: onomatopoeia*, metaphor*, symbol*, connotation*, metonymy*, personification*, pun* (lexical level); simile* (syntactical level); example* (compositional level).

instructive text (II) aims to give systematic directions on usage, action, or behaviour.

interior monologue (III) a lst person narrator reveals the protagonist's* psyche using complete sentences, a logically structured arrangement of ideas, and dealing with a coherent set of themes. There is a close relationship between reader and protagonist.

interpretation (introduction) attempt to reconstruct the author's original intention by means of a textual analysis on the basis of sociological, economic, cultural, biographical, psychological data; in most instances the critic will have to make do with an 'approach' towards the 'real' message, esp. in fictional* texts, where the use of stylistic devices* opens up a number of ways of understanding a text.

introduction/exposition (II) usually consists of elements leading up to the main section of the respective text form by either describing the initial situation or prior facts and events, by introducing themes, characters*, or theories. The exposition, a term reserved for fictional* texts, presents the initial setting*, action and events, and characters*. This part is sometimes dispensed with.

leitmotif (V) a dominant recurrent theme (word, phrase, emotion, idea) associated with a certain idea, person, or situation and accompanying its/her/his reappearance throughout the text.

limited point of view (III) the narrator* is a protagonist* in the story. He is limited in his knowledge to what he can possibly be aware of without violating the rules of probability. If the narrator is the main protagonist the point of view is that of a central consciousness*; if otherwise, that of a minor character*.

metaphor (V) a reduced or implied comparison between phenomena not normally associated with each other but having essential characteristics in common.

methods of characterisation (IV) in *showing** the character* can either present himself in a monologue, in a dialogue on a certain problem, by the choice of language, or he can be described by others. In *telling** the narrator* describes a character from his omniscient point of view*.

metonymy (V) substitution of the object in question by a closely associated feature, a characteristic part, or a proper name.

middle section (II) composite in character, it presents the description, reflection, action or argumentation essential to the text as a whole.

minor character (III) the narrator* is an unimportant character* who does not take an active part in the action himself but who views and evaluates everything from the stance of a witness on the periphery.

narrative text (II) makes statements about the action that takes place in a text.

narrator (III) mediator between a story and the reader; created to direct and influence the reception of the text. Author and narrator must be kept apart, are not interchangeable. A narrator can speak either in the first or the third person.

non-fictional text (I) its prime aim is to reflect as objectively as possible an aspect or aspects of the real world. Evaluative intervention is to be avoided at all costs; balance and neutrality should be the principal characteristics of the text, information its main purpose.

novel (I) long narrative which tries to present a fictional invented world in a comprehensive way, i.e. covering a long period of time and/or complex inner and outer conflicts. Usually sub-divided according to criteria of content (e.g. crime fiction, science fiction novel, love story, etc.).

objectivity (I) complete objectivity of presentation is impossible, as the element of personal selection already distorts absolute objectivity (as e.g. in newspaper reports, documentaries, history books); the effect on the reader can be manipulative.

omniscient or unlimited point of view (III) the narrator* has an unlimited knowledge of everything that has ever happened or will happen, about his characters*, their motivations and feelings. He does not participate in the story himself but views it from the outside, while commenting and evaluating.

onomatopoeia (V) sound(s) imitative of the thing(s) they refer to.

oxymoron (V) combination of two terms which are contradictory in meaning.

paradox (V) seemingly self-contradictory or absurd statement which in fact establishes a more complex level of meaning by way of association.

personification (V) reference to inanimate objects, abstract concepts or living beings (animals, plants) as if they were human beings with human attributes and qualities.

plot (IV) the logical, causal construction of setting*, action, characters* in a text* as opposed to the merely chronological arrangement of these components.

poetry (I) text form which is based on the condensed use of language and its distinctly identifiable outward appearance (line, stanza). Sub-grouping is possible according to structure (sonnet, ode, ballad, etc.) or content (love, war, nature, etc.).

point of view (III) refers to the way a story is told, i.e. to the modes of presenting the characters*, action, setting*, and events of a narrative. They differ according to the degree of insight the narrator* imparts to the reader, by either telling* or showing* him what he knows as an omniscient narrator*, a central consciousness*, a minor character*, or eliminated narrator*.

protagonist (IV) the main character* in a text, often contrasted with another character, the antagonist, in a conflict*.

pun (V) a humorous play on words which are either identical or similar in sound but different in meaning.

repetition/variation (V) the following terms belong to this group of stylistic devices* based on the identical or modified recurrence of text items: alliteration* (lexical); accumulation*, parallelism*, anaphora* (syntactical); leitmotif*, climax* (compositional).

reported thought (III) a 3rd person narrator* reveals the thoughts and feelings of the protagonist* in some form of the past tense. This form creates a certain distance between reader and protagonist.

rhetorical question (V) an assertion in the form of a question which strongly suggests a particular response.

round character (IV) a character* that is complex in temperament and motivation, capable of development and of changing his moral and ethical attitudes.

setting (IV) time, place, and environment in which the characters* move and the events take place.

shorter fiction (I) narratives such as the short story, fable, novella, etc. which concentrate on one significant aspect of life, thus not being able to present anything other than a limited view of the world ('slice of life'); most often they depict a crisis leading to a turning point.

showing (III/IV) the narrator* is practically absent (eliminated*) and the reader has to infer all the relevant information from the events as they unfold and from what the characters* say and do.

simile (V) an explicit comparison (using *as* or *like*) between two distinctly different things which have at least one feature in common.

stream of consciousness (III) a lst person narrator presents the protagonist's* state of mind in grammatically distorted sentences, connecting the apparently erratic thoughts by means of association rather than logic. In this way an almost complete identification between the reader and the protagonist is possible.

stylistic devices (V) used to increase or broaden meaning, to exaggerate, understate, or manipulate, to entertain or provide aesthetic pleasure, often by deviating from the basic conventions of communication*. The greater the density of stylistic devices in a text, the greater the likelihood of different interpretations* and appreciations of this text. Misunderstandings often result from misjudging the tone of a text. The main stylistic devices can be grouped together according to the functions of repetition/variation*, contrast*, imagery/analogy* and according to whether they are located on a lexical, syntactical, or compositional level.

symbol (V) denotes a concrete thing that stands for s.th. immaterial or abstract.

telling (III/IV) the narrator* knows everything (omniscient*) about the characters* and events of a story and imparts his knowledge to the reader, i.e. tells him about the motives and dispositional qualities of his characters or about what will happen.

text (introduction) arrangement of words and sentences which form a meaningful whole with respect to content, composition, language and evaluation.

text category (I) classification of texts according to their degree of truthfulness and objectivity* into fictional*, factional* and non-fictional* texts.

text form (I) sub-group of texts within the basic text categories* determined by formal, structural criteria (novel*, drama*), by their functional purpose (advertisement) or by the reference to their content (weather report).

text structure (II) composition* of a text in a number of interrelated sections, the three main sections being the introductory*, the middle*, and the final*, sections.

text type (II) classification of texts according to their intention into descriptive*, narrative*, expository*, argumentative*, and instructive* texts.

tone (V) the speaker's/author's attitude towards a text's subject, towards its readers and towards himself. This attitude can be ironic, sarcastic, humorous, angry, polemical, etc.

Stichwortregister
zum raschen Auffinden geeigneter Redemittel

ein ähnliches ***Stichwort*** *haben Sie im Kopf, in diese Richtung wollen Sie sich ausdrücken*

auf dieser ***Seite*** *finden Sie*

unter dieser ***Nummer*** *mögliche Redemittel dazu*

abschweifen 34 13
Absicht 48 22; **84** 12, 20
abwägen 34 15
analysieren 63 21; **84** 9
Argumentation 12 10; **34** 16; **83** 3; **84** 10; (~sstrang) **33** 10
Aspekt 13 19
Aufbau 12 11; **33** 1, 2, 3; **34** 20; **84** 14, 16, 19
aufdecken, bloßlegen 62 1
aufgreifen 12 16; **34** 12
Ausgangspunkt 33 7
Bedeutung 84 13, 15
beeinflussen 48 19
begründen 12 14
behandeln 33 9
beinhalten 48 20; **62** 14
Beispiel 12 13; **34** 16
Beschreibung 48 16; (einer Person) **62** 9–14
bestehen aus 33 3; **34** 18
betonen, hervorheben 12 12
sich **beziehen** auf **48** 20
bildhaft 83 2
beim Thema **bleiben 34** 14
Charakterisierung 62 1, 2, 3, 7–13, 16, 17, 18; **63** 24, 25
darlegen 34 11, 17
darstellen 33 5, 6, 9
einen **Eindruck** vermitteln **62** 15; **63** 23
Einleitung 33 5; **48** 20
entwickeln, darlegen 34 17
Entwicklung (einer Person) **62** 4, 5, 6
Erzähler 47 1–5; **48** 6–11, 19
Erzählweise 48 22; **62** 7

mit einem Thema **fortfahren 34** 14
fortschreiten 34 12
handeln von 12 3, 4; **48** 20
Hauptteil 34 12
hervorheben 12 12
bei näherem **Hinsehen 12** 15
Höhepunkt 34 20
karikieren 62 19
Klassifizierung 12 1, 2
Kontrastierung 34 16
sich **konzentrieren** auf **13** 19; **48** 16, 17
Parteinahme 12 7, 8, 9; **47** 3; **48** 11, 19
Perspektive 12 17; **48** 21 (Erzähl~) **47** 1, 4, 5; **48** 6–10
Realitätsbezug 12 6; **47** 3; **48** 11, 19
abschließen 34 19
Schluß 34 18, 19
schrittweise 33 8
Stellungnahme 34 18
Stereotyp 62 20
Stil 84 11
Stilmittel 84 9, 10, 12, 15, 17–23
Struktur 33 1, 3–8
Überschrift 33 4 (zur Strukturierung) **13** 18
überzeugen 12 10
untermauern, unterstreichen 34 16; **83** 3
untersuchen 33 1; **84** 9
variieren 34 13
Vergleich 34 16; **84** 10
verwenden, anwenden 83 1, 2
Wirkung 84 12, 15, 17–20
zurückkehren zu ..., wieder aufgreifen 12 16; **34** 12
Zusammenfassung 34 19

Acknowledgements

Text	Source
Chapter I	
1	Brian Morris, "Weekend Telegraph" in: *Daily Telegraph*, 29 October 1965
2	James Thurber, *The Thurber Carnival*, re. Harmondsworth: Penguin Books 1965
3	Edward Albee, "The Zoo Story" in: *Absurd Drama*, re. Harmondsworth: Penguin Books 1976

4 Carl Sandburg, "The Hangman at Home" in: *Harvest Poems 1910–1960*, New York: Harcourt, Brace + World, Inc. 1960
5 Lord Tweedsmuir, *The Country Life Picture Book of Scotland*, London 1977
6 Bertrand Russell, *Great Essays in Science*, ed. by M. Gardner, Pocket Library. Original: The New York Times Magazine 19 March 1950
7 Martin Luther King, "I have a dream" quoted from: King, M. L., *Broadside Records Album No. 592*, New York: Broadside Records 1964
8 *The Times*, 29 July 1983
9 *The Guardian*, 23 February 1984
10 *New Statesman*, 9 December 1983
11 Catherine Hughes, *American Playwrights 1945–75*, London: Pitman Publishing 1976
12 From "An Introduction to Science", in: *Listen to leaders in science*, Atlanta 1965
13 *The Times*, 29 July 1983
14 Matsushita Electric Trading Co., Ltd.
15 Reinhard Kemnitz

Chapter II
1 see I,2
2 Langston Hughes, "Early Autumn" from *Black Short Story Anthology*, ed. Woodie King, New York: Columbia Univ. Press 1972
3 R. D. Laing, "How can she be happy" from R. D. Laing, *Knots* re., London: Tavistock Publications 1971
4 Tom Sharpe, *Vintage Stuff*, London: Pan Books 1983
5 In: Albert Rowe, *Language Matters*, Exeter: A. Wheaton and Co., Ltd. 1977
6 *New Society*, 7 June 1984
7 *Psychology Today*, June 1978
8 *Psychology Today*, November 1978
9 Michael Carrier and The Centre for British Teachers, *Take 5, Games and Activities for the Language Learner*, London 1980
10 *Encyclopaedia Britannica* Inc., Chicago 1981

Chapter III
1 Henry Fielding, *The History of Tom Jones. A Foundling*, re., London and Glasgow: Collins 1964
2 Dr. D. J. Hessayon, *The House Plant Expert* Waltham Cross, Herts.: pbi Publications, Britannica House 1980
3 William Shakespeare, *Romeo and Juliet*, The Arden Edition, London and New York: Methuen 1980
4 Jane Austen, "Sense and Sensibility" in: *The Complete Novels of Jane Austen*, Random House, Inc.
5 Alan Sillitoe, *The Loneliness of the Long-Distance Runner*, re., London: W. H. Allen 1982
6 Eudora Welty, "A Visit of Charity" in: *A Curtain of Green*, New York: Harcourt Brace & Co. 1941
7 James Joyce, *A Portrait of the Artist as a Young Man*, re., Harmondsworth: Penguin 1970
8 Thomas Hardy, "A Tradition of Eighteen Hundred and Four" in: *Wessex Tales*, London: Macmillan 1982

9 *The Observer,* 3 July 1983
10 Ernest Hemingway, "Hills like White Elephants" in: *The Essential Hemingway,* Harmondsworth: Penguin 1973
11 *Sunday Times,* 2 January 1983
12 William Shakespeare, *Macbeth,* London: Oxford University Press 1964
13 Alun Lewis, "The Lapse" in: *The Last Inspection,* London: George Allen & Unwin Ltd.
14 James Joyce, *Ulysses,* re., Harmondsworth: Penguin 1976

Chapter IV
1 Arnold Wesker, *Chips With Everything,* London: Jonathan Cape 1962
2 *New Statesman,* 10 August 1984
3 Agatha Christie, *The Mysterious Affair at Styles,* John Lane the Bodley Head Ltd. 1920
4 Nigel Williams, *Class Enemy,* re., London: Methuen 1981
5 William Golding, *Lord of the Flies,* re., London: Faber and Faber 1970
6 Peter Terson, *Zigger Zagger,* re., Harmondsworth: Penguin 1981
7 Charles Dickens, "A Christmas Carol" in: *Christmas Books by Charles Dickens,* London: Oxford University Press 1970
8 *The Observer,* 16 September 1984
9 Erskine Caldwell, "Saturday Afternoon" in: *The Complete Stories by Erskine Caldwell,* Boston: Little, Brown and Co. 1941

Chapter V
1 Published by the International Communication Agency, Embassy of the United States of America
2 same as above
3 in A. Norman Jeffares (Ed.), *Poems of W. B. Yeats,* re., London: MacMillan 1971
4 *The New English Bible,* Harmondsworth: Penguin 1974
5 Chatto & Windus Ltd.
6 *New Statesman,* 14 October 1983
7 *The Observer,* 2 October 1983
8 William Shakespeare, *Julius Caesar,* The Arden Edition, re., London: Methuen 1977
9 Pink Floyd, *The Wall,* EMI Electrola 1979
10 for Yeats see reference to text V,3; for Shakespeare see reference to text III,3; *The Advanced Learner's Dictionary of Current English,* 2nd ed., London: Oxford University Press 1963
11 *The Times,* 27 September 1983
12 Ted Hughes, *Selected Poems 1957–1967,* re., London: Faber & Faber 1979
13 Rupert Hart-Davis Ltd., London